FRAMEWORK OF PUBLIC POLICY

FRAMEWORK OF PUBLIC POLICY

THE DISCIPLINE AND ITS DIMENSIONS

DR. P. B. RATHOD
Reader
Dept. of Political Science
Gulbarga University
Gulbarga-585106
Karnataka (India)

Commonwealth

Framework of Public Policy : The Discipline and Its Dimensions

1st Edition : 2005
ISBN 81-7169-950-2

Published by :
Commonwealth Publishers
4831/24, Prahlad Street,
Ansari Road, Darya Ganj,
New Delhi - 110002
Phone : 23272541, 23257835
Fax : 91-011-23257835
e-mail : campusbooks@hotmail.com

Laser Typesetting by :
Stylish Laser Typesetter
Delhi

Printed at :
Roshan Offset Printers
Delhi

FOREWORD

Public policy is emerging as an inter-disciplinary and as such it is concerned with the application of scientific means and methods for solving the public problems. Public policy is a new subject and as such it is regarded as the part and parcel of public administration. Policy is very essential in administration for it gives concrete shape to the political, economic and social objectives which the government lays down in the form of laws, rules and regulations.

Coming at this crucial theme is the book entitled *"Framework of Public Policy : The Discipline and Its Dimensions* authored by Dr. P. B. Rathod, Reader, Dept. of Political Science, Gulbarga University, Gulbarga. In the opening chapter the learned author has systematically and scientifically explained the meaning, nature and objectives of public policy. In the second chapter the eminent scholar is devoted for the analysis of the Approaches and Models of Public Policy. Policy and environment have been comprehensively brought out in the third chapter of the book. The Author has made a penetrating explanation about the policy formulation in the fourth chapter of the treatise. Chapter fifth and sixth is completely dedicated for the policy implementation and policy evaluation respectively.

In toto this book on the "Framework of Public Policy : The Discipline and Its Dimensions" is a very comprehensive, systematic and authoritative analysis of the various facts and figures of the public policy. The work is well documented and researched by appropriate support of notes and references. The author has put down his enormous experience as a teacher of this subject for the last 17 years in the form of a well planned volume. The language used is simple, lucid, clear and intelligible to the students. It is also a treatise worth keeping in the study of serious scholars of Public Administration, Economics, Geography and other Social Sciences. The author, whom I know from the very close quarters and respect as a scholar of great eminence in the field of Political Science has spared no efforts and taken all pains in structuring such a massive work.

Therefore, this treatise is an undoubtful addition of garland of pearls in the rich treasure of political science and public policy of our country. I am sure that it will be viewed as a landmark in the field and commend as a useful source material for advanced learning. I wish the venture all the success.

Subhash V. Rathod
Academic Council Member
G.U.G.

PREFACE

We often make references to the various policies of the government and attempt to evaluate those from our own points of consideration. Public policy is an important branch of public administration. In other words, it is the part and parcel of public administration. Public policies are the ones with which all living beings in a political system are concerned. The individuals in a given set-up can be divided into two categories from the public policies point of view. First are those who are benefited by the policy, and the second are the ones who are loosers. Public policies possess the attributes to attract the attention of both these types of individuals, therefore, normally all have their eyes fixed on the policies. The interest-factor increases the anxiety and concern of even common man towards the public policies enacted and implemented. The public policies are goals oriented. The major task of any government is to formulate and enact the policies whereby the developmental targets fixed, in accordance to the needs and circumstances, are achieved or attained. The governments are active in the policy development at all levels—national, state, and local with the sole motive of providing programmes which could be of the public benefits at large.

Like politics, public policies are unescapable and so are its consequences. Policies play a vital role in shaping and re-shaping the lives of the people in a given political structure. Public Policies are the focal point of politics in political system. Policies are the goals or purposes of government programmes. It does include the implementation of intentions and rules. It can be termed explicitly in rules or implicitly in actions and schedules. Normally, public policies, are the governmental rules and programmes, considered individually or collectively, that is, the authoritative decisional output of the political system. Public Policies are expressed in a variety of forms including laws, local ordinances, court decisions, executive orders etc. Policy making process is a part of politics and political action. The power, control, bargaining and gaming concepts have an important role in the enactment of public policies.

Policy formulation and implementation are the important facets of politics and administration to be pondered over seriously by the scholars of public administration and political science. With the aid of various models for policy analysis, and attempt can be made to analyse and evaluate the policies made by the government and its suitability and impact on the masses. The present work endeavours to highlight various conceptual dimensions of public policy process. There have been few works earlier also on public policy them by the Indian scholars. The author feel satisfied in collectively bringing out all the theoretical and practical dimensions in the field of public policy. The present work would be of great help and assistance to the students, teachers, and researchers/scholars in the disciplines of public administration and political science. Moreover, it would also be of the interest to the general readers, who want to know about various issues and approaches involved in policy making process. The book is divided into six chapters and has a detailed bibliography at the end. The public policies have great and quantitative influence of the ecological and environmental factors and forces. The public policy formulation and implementation and environment has been paid substantial attention in this book. How an issue emerges as a public issue and catches the attention of the policy makers and the long distance it has to cover for actually becoming a public policy has been thoroughly analysed and discussed. The policy formulated is of no use unless it is appropriately implemented and enforced. There are certain problems faced by the implementors for executing the policies. The implementation process of the policies has been dealt with in details. Finally, the policies made have to be evaluated in order to improve, amend, or abolish the policies. The evaluation part is equally important in the policy-making process. Hence, it has been discussed in length.

The brief outline of the contents of the chapters is as follows.

In the first chapter, that is public policy, the politics-policy relationship, public policy has been defined at length from the writings of Aristotle upto the present times. The stages, objectives, the functional aspects of the political system, the basis, dilemmas and the types of public policy are also included in this chapter.

The second chapter, under the heading Approaches and Models of Public Policy, contains basis components, issues of policy analysis. Furthermore twelve models and also utility of public policy have been discussed in details.

The third chapter, entitled Public Policy and Environment includes in detail the Governmental and the non-Governmental policy making agencies.

Chapter fourth, under the heading Policy Formulation, contains discussion on Identification of policy problems, setting up of an agenda to make policies, Bureaucracy-executive, Executive-Legislature and Legislature-Bureaucracy interactions regarding policy formulations and different decision-making styles.

The fifth chapter, Policy Implementation, includes analysis of the role of policy Implementors such as the legislature, the courts, the pressure groups, the administrative agencies. It also deals with the requirements of implementation of policies and the public support and cooperation in getting the policies executed.

The last chapter, Policy Evaluation, contains discussions about the ways and means through which the policies are evaluated, and how the impacts of the policies are measured and determined. The limitations of public policy have also been discussed in this chapter.

Finally, there is bibliography having around six hundred references and articles of public policy and on the themes related to it.

I am greatly indebted to my parents for their encouragement to complete this work. My sincere thanks are due to Prof. V.B. Coutinho, Vice-Chancellor, Gulbarga University, Gulbarga for his constant encouragement and moral support in academic activities.

I am grateful to my young, dynamic and enthusiastic publisher, Shri Ajay Verma, Proprietor, Commonwealth Publishers, New Delhi for bringing out this valuable book in time.

It has throughout been very kind an considerate of my wife, Vimala, for extending me full co-operation during the preparation of manuscripts drafts a number of times. I feel highly obliged to her.

I am sure there may be few shortcomings in this book. I make an earnest appeal to the readers to appraise me of those, so that I can improve the work on the basis of their much cared for suggestions.

Dr. P. B. Rathod
Reader
Dept. of Political Science
G.U.G.

CONTENTS

Foreword (*v*)
Preface (*vii*)

Chapter *Pages*

1. Public Policy—Meaning, Nature and Types 1
2. Approaches and Models of Public Policy 47
3. Public Policy and Environment 74
4. Policy Formulation 109
5. Policy Implementation 137
6. Policy Evaluation 160

Bibliography 182
Index 216

1

PUBLIC POLICY—MEANING, NATURE AND TYPES

Public policy is emerging as an interdisciplinary field of inquiry and as such it is concerned with the application of scientific methods and insights to the improvement of public policy making and the solution to public problems is policy science.[1] Policies may be thought of as the main system which provides the framework for the achievement of intended objectives. Formulation of policy involves making explicit the various assumptions which are made with respect to the basic premises and the priorities of needs and allocation of the finances accordingly. Besides, policies are intended to spell out the parameters in the context of which organisational decisions are to be made.[2] Policy is very essential in administration for it gives concrete shape to the political, economic and social objectives which the government lays down in the form of laws, rules, regulations etc.

Policies may be looked upon as general guides to action.[3] They may be verbal, written or implied. They set the overall boundaries for action by individuals or groups in an organisational setting. The indicate the framework within which executes may make decisions for the performance of organisational action.

Public policy represents primarily the applied as contrasted with the pure science aspects of relevant disciplines.[4] Given the wide range of public problems, policy scientists may be drawn from almost any discipline—social, biological, or physical. The disciplines most directly concerned with the policy sciences approach have been Political Science, Sociology, Law, Business Management, History and Public Administration. Policy Sciences also utilize insights drawn from such fields systems analysis, operation research, cybernetics, game theory and general systems theory, which cut across traditional disciplinary boundaries. Policy Scientists are particularly concerned with the process of clarifying goals, evaluating alternatives, identifying trends and analyzing the policy situation. It does not concerned only the basic values, but, rather is concerned with factual propositions that are subject to empirical inquiry. Nevertheless, the policy scientists contribute to goal choice by rendering judgement on the feasibility of means, the range of possible choices and the possible consequences of alternative choices.[5]

Basic concept of state has drastically changed from the past to the present times. In the past states were small and they were called as 'police' states; and their duty was the maintenance of law and order and the collection of the revenue.[6] But modern states are welfare states, and their activities are expanding by leaps and bounds. Public welfare is the main goal of modern states.[7] Infact, state has always been the product of social Economic and political environments and circumstances. Now-a-days states affects and influences and is being affected and influenced by its environment. Both influences each other. Right from Aristotle (Father of Political Science) to Karl Marx (Founder of Communism), it is clearly reflected that environments have influenced the philosophers for considerably moulding their thinking and philosophy.[8] A public policy is commonly known as the relationship to the governmental units to its environment therefore, it becomes imperative to take into account the depiction governments made by various prominent political thinkers.

Aristotle was the first to make an attempt to classify states.[9] His classification was qualitative as well as quantitative. From quantity he meant the number of persons who were in power, whereas, from quality the meant whether those in power worked for collective welfare or looked after their selfish interests. If it was in the interest of the community, the form of government was normal, pure otherwise it was perverted or impure. As per him, Monarchy, Aristocracy and polity were normal forms of government, whereas their corresponding perverted forms were Tyranny, Oligarchy and Democracy. He believed that the governments always moved in circle.[10] He stressed on the system of direct democracy which eventually meant denial of contraction of powers in the hands of executive government.

Diagram of the Classification of Government

Number of Rulers	*Pure Form*	*Impure Form*
Rule by one	Monarchy	Tyranny
Rule of few	Aristocracy	Oligarchy
Rule by Many	Polity	Democracy

Polybins adopted ethical, normative and moral basis for the purpose of classifying states. He held the view that the king was justified to rule when his commands were spontaneously obeyed by his objects. The king should be loved and not feared.[11]

Hobbes, a great empiricist, individualist, the well known exponent of the social-contract philosophy, believed that there was no permanent, normal or perverted form of government. He was of the view that whether a form of government was normal or perverted depended on the suitability of conditions or requirements of people on whom it was being imposed.[12] Those who loved one man rule called it monarchy and it was the normal form of government for them, whereas, for others it was tyranny and thus perverted. John Locke also contributed to the ideas of Hobbes. He however, held the opinion that the forms of governments were monarchy, oligarchy and democracy. When the power vested in the hands of one man it was monarchy, which could be hereditary as well as elected. It was oligarchy when the few selected governed a nation.

According to Montesquieu, if power was vested in the hands of masses it was republic, may be democratic or aristocratic. In monarchy, monarch rules for collective welfare whereas in despotism power is misused for promoting and protecting selfish interests.[13] Rousseau also attempted to classify state and governments into Monarchies, Aristocracies and Democracies. He was however, champion of democratic form of government. He held the view that all other forms of government were just subordinate to the democratic government.

Herbert Spencer compared state organism with individual organism by saying that as organs of individual were interdependent on each other, so were the organs of the state.[14] All organs of the state, like those of human beings, are supposed to work in close collaboration with each other. According to him, "As is the relation of the hand to the body or the leaf to the tree, so is the relation of the man to the society. He exists in it and it in him.

Austin was of the opinion that the best form of government was one in which a determinate human superior was given constant and willing obedience by the bulk of the society but such obedience was, however, not the product of fear. He believed that in all circumstances the sovereign must be obeyed. In fact, according to him, the welfare of the society depended in giving unqualified obedience to the sovereign.[15]

T.H. Green held the view that an ideal state was one which gave greatest, happiness to maximum number of people. The state should promote collective pleasure and happiness[16]. Psychologically, every individual loves happiness and pleasure and remove all those factors which directly or indirectly promote fear. According to Karl Marx, a perfect and true state would be one which would emerge on the debris of the present state and in which the capitalists will no longer exploit the poors and none will live on the labour of others, but every one will get as per his needs and requirements.[17]

After having a glimpse of the state of affairs in operation even during the ancient times as depicted through the views of various political thinkers, one thing becomes clear that depending upon the needs of the time and the environments around different types of governments—Aristocracy, Oligarchy, Monarchy, Tyranny, Mobocracy, Democracy, etc. were in existence at different times. Of course, depending upon the limited demands of the people and the human being, life being affected by individual or natural factors, there was no much scope for the governments at that time to ponder over the issues and policies to be formulated for the welfare of the masses. Neither that much qualitative and quantitative awareness was there among both the rulers and the ruled to bring out the schedules and programmes in the forms of public policies. Undoubtedly, the scope of the government was also very much limited in the ancient times. In accordance with the progress of civilization man's life was not only affected by nature but also by the social factors. Most important social factor is "Social Governance". It means administration at the various levels, *i.e.*, District State and Central Administration. Such an administration or the government is established by the individuals in the society to solve their increasing problems of law and order, transport, inflation and depression, safety measures, education, unemployment etc. Now we are not residing in the city states where we had limited problems and demands, we are now in the national and rather international states and in this supersonic age our problems and demands have increased to such a considerable extent that for solving those problems and fulfilling the demands, the governments—whether Democratic, Monarhic, Aristocratic, Military rule—have to make many policies. These policies made by the government are known as public policies.[18] When we are travelling in state transport bus, which is jam packed, and we are sweating profusely, at that time we are directly or indirectly under the effect of one public policy or the other.

The public policies are those which are formulated by the governmental bodies and officials and sometimes even the non-governmental agents and actors also play an important role in this direction.[19] Public policies are the governmental rules and programmes, considered individually or collectively, that is, the authoritative decisional output of the political system. Public policy may be expressed in a variety of forms, including laws, local ordinances, court decisions, executive orders, decisions and administrators or even unwritten understanding of what is to be done. Policy without the modifies public is sometimes regarded as synonymous with governmental decision, but it is often treated as embracing a set or sequence of decisions rather than a single decision about a specific governmental action. Policy is also termed by some to distinguish decisions about goals or preferences from decisions relating to the means of achieving goals. Others, however, may treat policy as embracing both ends and means. Policy in some contexts refers to decisions about long-range objectives or general directions of governmental action which serves as guides to short-run action in specific cases.[20] Policies are the goals or purposes of government programmes for example, the eradication of poverty, better employment opportunities fool proof safety measures.[21] Policy does include the implementation of intentions and rules. Policy can be termed explicity in rules or implicity in actions and schedules. Policies to provide the standard guides which facilitate planning and acting in a line with legal requirements to realise the predetermined goals and objectives. The executive in political system is helped by the policies in keeping its activites within the prescribed framework of action. There is a close relationship between politics and policy. It is the politics only which leads to the enactment of policies. When the political system is viewed from the politics point of consideration, one finds the demands made by the masses upon the government officials or the party in power. These demands bring out the emergence of the policies.[22] Policies have a substantial bearing on the minds of the people. Supposing the policies of a government are not in tune with the demands of the time, the people who enjoy the ultimate power of electing the government in democracies can change the party in the next elections. A typical example to this effect can be noted of the proclamation of internal emergency in India by Indira Gandhi's government in 1975. Masses did not approve of it and the result was clear, the Congress Party headed by Indira Gandhi was badly routed out in January 1977 elections. Again when the Janata government could not depict absolute unity among themselves during 1977-1979, people voted the party out of power in 1980 midterm polls. Hence, the effect of policies on the minds of the inhabitants cannot be minimised.

Policy making process is a part of politics and political action.[23] The power control, bargaining and gaming concepts play a significant role in the enactment of public policies. There are values studies about public policy and the authors have attempted to define public policy from different angles. But keeping in view the substantial significance, the field is having, the studies made are not much in number. Large number of political scientists have explored the political processes and contexts in which those occur, but on the subject of public policy not that much amount of work and research on scientific mode of investigation has been carried out. A major reason for this is obviously overt value content of public policy questions and the temptation, therefore, of any citizen, professional political scientist, public administrate or not, comment on such questions.

Definitions of Public Policy

Robert Eye Stone terms public policy as "the relationship of government unit to its environment."[24] The definition given by Robert Eye Stone is the one which is highly vague and complex. It does not make the things amply clear to all the persons. Had he defined what does it mean by environment to which the governmental unit is to have its relationships, the things might have been more clear because environment as such is a very vast term. It is the setting or surrounding conditions within which any object, activity, or system occurs.[25] The environment of a political system includes human and non-human factors, both tangible and intangible. Thus, for example, geographical factors, other social systems, ideologies, customs and institutions may all be features of the environment of a political system. In systems analysis, the environment consists of all phenomena that affect the functioning of the system and that are not part of the system.

Thomas R. Dye says that, "Public policy is whatever government chooses to do or not to do." The words of Thomas R. Dye do not seem to precise upto considerable extent. There can be a major division between what government chooses to do and what it actually does. Simply by keeping certain important priority areas in view does not serve the purpose, unless some concrete action is taken on those.

Richard Rose says that "Public policy is not a decision, it is a course or pattern of activity." This sounds to be somewhat nearer to the reality. Public policy formulation and implementation involves R. well planned pattern or course of activity. Just by deciding one fine morning, that a particular policy should be made will not let the issue resolved. Public policy process requires a thoroughly close knit relation and interaction between the important governmental agencies, *viz.* the executive, legislature, bureaucracy and judiciary.[26]

In Carl J. Iriedrich's opinion public policy "is a proposed course of action of a person, group or government within a given environment providing opportunities and obstacles which the policy was proposed to utilize and overcome in an effort to reach a goal or realize an objective or purpose." Friedrich has given an exhaustive analysis of the meaning of public policy. We find combination of the view points of Robert Eye Stone and Richard Rose in the words of Friedrich. He has taken positive points of the definitions of public policy made by Robert Eye Stone and Richard Rose. He has attempted to confine the environment and has termed public policy as a line or course of action adopted by the individual group and government for facilitating the public policy process and doing away with the stambling blacks in its way for the attainment of objectives and accomplishment of goals.[27]

The above stated definitions of public policy by various authors and an analysis of those definitions can be concluded as such :

1. Public policies are goal oriented[28]. In order to attain the objects which the government has in view for the ultimate benefit of the masses in general, the public policies are formulated and implemented. These are the ones which are value laden and speal of the programme of the government in action overtly.
2. Public policy is a pattern or course of activity of the governmental officials and actors collectively rather than being termed as their discrete and segregated decisions.
3. Public policy is what government actually decides or chooses to do and is the relationship of the government units to the specific field of political environment is a given administrative system.[29]
4. Public policy is positive in the sense that it depicts the concern of the government and involves its action to a particular problem on which the policy is made. Negatively, it involves a decision by governmental actors not to take any action on a particular issue.
5. Public policy, in its positive form has the sanction of law and authority behind it, and that is why, it is called as authoritative.
6. Public policy stems from a well defined procedure wherein the power control, gaming and bargaining concepts play a significant role.

The preceding analysis reveals that public policy is a goal oriented action of the government. It is clearly defined course of action adopted by the political agencies and actors in the line to achieve certain goals.

Nature of Public Policy

Public policy has been termed as a pattern or course of activity and as the relationship of the government unit to its environment[30]. Public policy is based upon policy demands and claims made upon public official by other actors, governmental or non-governmental in a given political system for taking some action to sort out a specific programme. The action taken by the governmental actors and agencies pertaining to any issue is known as policy decision. The policy decision helps the governmental officials to provide direction and content to public policy actions. Their action to the effect is based on the formal expressions or articulations of public policies. This formal expression or articulation is termed as policy statement and it includes all legislative states executive orders and decrees, and administrative rules and regulations in it. Public policy is often analysed in the light of the outputs of the policy decision or statement. Policy outputs are the tangible manifestation of the public policies. In simple words, policy outputs reflect what has actually been done by the government. The net result of the public policy is viewed by considering the outcomes of the policy. How many have been benefited and how many are the losers and in how much quality and quantity and what are the overall. Consequences of the policy are the normal questions the public policy is being put.

Public policies depict the overall functioning of a political system. The operational area of public policy is abundantly vast and its range and scope thoroughly wide.[31] Let us take any aspect of the human life we just cannot escape from one public policy or the other. Right from the birth of the child upto death of a man even when the dead body is taken to grave yard for final rites, there is some policy or the other we are facing and taking benefits of. Education of the child, prevention from diseases, better and nutritious meals good clothes, best higher education, job potentials, better salaries adequate housing facilities, safety from national or international dangers, safety from natural calamities are some of the policies we can easily talk about. Keeping in view the interdependence on other national powers, the public policies of a political system also do include in them policies pertaining to import and export aspects and good and cordial relations with other nations. It is rather difficult to restrict or define the scope and range of public policy in words.

Stages of Public Policy

It has been mentioned earlier that public policy is not a

decision, but a pattern or course of activity. Hence it has to pass through certain stages which are as follows :

1. *Policy Formulation* : The first stage in public policy process is policy formulation. Public policy is a proposed course of action dealing with public demands and problems. As per input-output model of Gabrial A. Almond the demands are converted into policies with the aid of input, *i.e.*, factors like political socialization, interest aggregation, interest articulation and political communication. These input factors convert the demands into outputs which include Rule making, Rule interpreting and Rule enforcing. According to the Feed back model of David Easton, the demands of the people which are not converted into policies are again fed through the same procedure till the action is taken on those. At the policy formulation a close knit relationship between executive-legislature, Bureaucracy-executive and Bureaucracy-Legislature gets revealed.[32]

2. *Policy Interpretation* : Once the policy is formulated, the policy includes number of technical words and phrases. The interpretation of such terms and phrases is very important to be given, otherwise wrong meaning of the policy can be taken up. Therefore, it becomes imperative on the part of governmental actors to interpret the policy.[33]

3. *Policy Education* : The next stage in the public policy process is policy education. The government through various channels of mass media attempts to make masses aware of the policy made by it. It is very much necessary to educate public about the policy because people will obey and respect it only when they will come to understand it.

4. *Policy Implementation* : After the policy is framed or formulated, interpretated and the masses educated about it, the next phase or stage is that of policy implementation. This is also a very crucial stage, because unless and until the policies are properly and positively implemented, it will of no use to spend time on their formulation. The mented, it will be of no use to spend time on their formulation. The implementation

work is mainly undertaken by the various administrative agencies operating at all the levels—Central, State and Local.[34]

5. *Policy Control* : The last phase of the policy process is control over the public policies formulated and implemented by the various governmental actors and agencies. It is the duty of the government to exercise full control on public policies so that the purpose for which the policies have been made is achieved and the masses get the due benefits out of the some. Proper and appropriate adjudicative and administrative functions are required for keeping complete control over the public policies.

Objectives of Public Policy

Public policy is a set of code of conduct of a political system on lines of which the governmental functions are performed. In a democratic set up government is nothing but a reflection of society as a whole. Government has various fields of administration like education, defence, health, finance etc. For every field or for a particular area the government formulates policies commonly known as public policies. But at the time of formulation of policies some objectives are determined which ought to be achieved at the end. Various factors influence in the determination of objectives.[35] While doing so, some point are kept in view-objectives should be scientific, realistic and help in advancement of the society and welfare of the general masses. Objectives are determined to suit the basic and dire needs of the society in totality. In democratic policy, different political parties contest elections with an aim to come to power. At the same time of the election the political parties place before the public, lists of their policies and programmes in the shape of election manifestos. The party which comes to power normally takes into account the promises it had made with the electorate at the time of election, and hence attempts to make policies in accordance to that for achieving the objectives.

Types of Objectives

The various objectives of public policy are mentioned below :

1. *Long Term Objectives* : If the policy is for long term then the objectives will also be determined likewise. For example, in a defence policy long term objectives are kept in view. These can be pertaining to meritorious recruitment, adequate training, proper armament etc. Similarly policies on education, economy, health and family welfare etc. would be having objectives determined on long term basis.[36]

2. *Short Term Objectives* : Some of the problems emerge by chance. In such cases, policies are formulated with objectives on short term basis.[37] For example, at the time of war, blackouts are ordered and people are withdrawn from the villages near the border areas. Similarly, if violence breaks down somewhere policy with short term objectives will be made to restore law and order over there.

Sometimes certain policies also influence the determination of objectives of the same or another policy. For example, the outcome of the family planning programme of the Congress-I during 1975-77 influenced the policy adopted by Janata government after 1977 in the same area to a considerable extent. The objective of the family planning policy is to check the population growth, the Congress-I forced the programme but the Janata government after seeing the reaction of the masses on the coercion used by the Congress-I government persuaded the masses to adopt the programme.

3. *Scientific Objectives* : Public policy can be studies in order to gain greater knowledge about its origin, the process by which it develops and its consequences for society. This is in turn increases our understanding of political system in particular and society in general. The policy may be regarded as a dependent valuable or independent valuable for purpose of such kind of analysis. When it is viewed as a dependent valuable our attention is placed on the political and environmental factors that help to determine the content of the policy. If public policy is viewed as an independent variable our focus shifts to the political system and its environment. Thus it reveals the overall working of the government and its concern for the masses.[38]

4. *Professional Objectives* : The knowledge gathered with the help of scientific tools and techniques is put to use for solving certain issues in a professional and well defined manner. The question over here is not whether the political scientists should endeavour clarifying the goals and attainments of public policy. The important aspect is that when we are conversant with the role played by certain factors in shaping the public policy then we can definitely say something relevant regarding the involvement of governmental actors or agencies, individuals and groups in attaining policy goals. It can amount to an indication regarding the requirements of certain policies for meeting the demand and the physical political and environmental factors needed for the same to be enacted and implemented.[39]

5. *Political Objectives* : It is the view of some political scientists that the public policy study should aim to the formulation of light type of policies being adopted by the governments for accomplishing appropriate goals. They aspire for better quality of public policy, notwithstanding that considerable disagreement prevails among people regarding the composition of correct policies or the right goals of policy.[40]

Politics and Policy

Politics is human activity concerned with making and implementing decisions vested with the authority of the society for which decisions are made. Politics refers to activity or process, whereas "Political System" implies the existence of structures or patterned relationships. On a practical setting, politics has been called the art of possible, the art of governing, and the study of who gets, what when and how. Sometimes politics is defined as the art of formulation and implementation of public policies. Prof. Morgenthau Said like all politics, international politics is a struggle for power! Politics is a means as to how to 'acquire power, retain power and expand power'. In other words, it is 'refined interms of power relationships.[41] It is both an art and science of government. To some people politics is the study of state, government and administration. It is nothing but a decision making process. Politics is both good and words. It is more worse than good. It is commonly identified with the exercise of influence, the struggle for power and competition among individuals and groups over the allocation of rewards or values within a society. It is also said to involve a social steering process, including the setting and attaining of collective goals.

The many faces of politics—the decision making, value-allocating, goal-setting, goal-steering, power-seeking, interest competing, influence-exerting activities may appear within any social group. In most political discourse, however, politics refers to public policies and allocation rather than the internal process of private organisations. A keen and thorough observation of political life made at the range and diversity of political actions can conclude that no single definition of politics may cover the entire range of political events. On the past, the political theorists has been defining politics in evaluative terms stating not only what politics is, but what it ought to be. It is the science of the state (H.C. James). Garner, for instance, described it as that study which "begins and ends with the state. On the past is politics 'State and government were the main focus.[42]

Modern View : Politics as an Activity : Contesting elections, propagating political ideologies, manning political offices, taking part in political parties and so on. If we are to look at politics, we would discover that it is a multi-stage activity involving a large number of people and it is performed endlessly. Politics as an instrument of social control : Politics is an instrument of social power and prestige, and a double-edged weapon both to derive gain to oneself and one's relations, friends and supporters, and to deny it to one's adversalies.[43] Politics as a game of power.[44] Politics is an instrument with the help of which we acquire power. In other words politics is the game of power. It occurs everywhere, from home to the international arena. Further politics involves some sort of power, rule and authority. But power is its central concern. The game of politics is also incomplete without caste power, money power and muscle power. Power gives authority. Power is the source of economic prosperity. Power confers on one a prestigious social status. Thus power is the be-end and be-all of politics.

The most commonly agreed definition of politics presently is that "politics is the authoritative allocation of values".[45] (David Easton). During mid-fifties, the discipline of political science was keenly looking towards a well established definition. At the time it was suggested that politics involves the authoritative allocation of values within a society. It was an attempt to identify the defining function of political life. It defined that all types of government, whether dictatorial or democratic, oligarchic or monarchic, are said to allocate values is an authoritative manner. The concept of authoritative allocation of values has conceptualized politics as a system of action with the defining function occupying the central place (Easton, 1953).

An emblematic system design for politics is as follows :

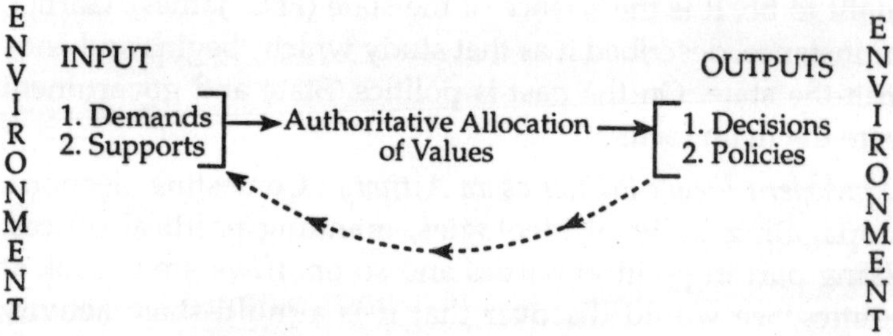

The above system design or diagram shows that the inputs in the form of demands and support become outputs in the shape of policies and decisions by the authoritative allocation of values. This is a kind of function which majority of the institutions can carry out. The issue which seeks the attention for resolving it is to precisely known-does the allocation of values appropriately define politics? We had started from the point that the politics was defined as the authoritative allocation of values. David Eston has termed policy as "authoritative" when people feel they must or ought to obey it. But he has no where mentioned about the situations when people would not like to obey the orders passed by the political masters in an authoritative manner. Human beings are the ones who have certain traditions and feelings and they seldom prefer to do away with those for the sake of authoritative values. In the strongest traditions of political life, social customs may govern behaviour more effectively than any overt directive from political leaders. In such like situations, policies are carried out from habit not from any feeling about what must or ought to be done.[45]

The second term "Allocation" used by David Easton in his definition of politics also does not fall in full conformity in explaining politics.[47] Does it mean that politics is always a kind of allocation. It is agreed that there are certain public policies by which the goods are allocated to the society, in the list can be included policies on social security, eradication of poverty, better payments and salaries, etc. but alongwith it are certain such kinds of policies also whereby no allocation of goods is made to the public. In this category can be listed policy on supply of public goods and policy on ethical issues. Other marginally allocationist policies are some regulatory policies as enforcement of Law and Order and reforms in the electoral system.

The third aspect of David Easton's definition is "values".[48] Value is a concept of what is desirable or good or, in some usages, the good or desired thing itself. Values may thus reflect what a person wants—a goal, a preference, a desired end state or they may reflect his concept of what is good and right, what he ought rather than what he wants to do. Values are internal, subjective concepts that postulate standards of morality, aesthetics and personal preference. Values through public policies can be allocated firstly by rearranging the attitudes of citizens that express values and secondly by distributing the things that are valued by citizens. In both the ways it is not that easy and swift for the government to come out successfully with its purpose.

The meaning of "Authoritative Allocation of Values" is explained with the example in the following way.

When sugar supply is sufficient, then there is no difficulty in getting it. But when it is short, there is a mad rush in getting it. When it is regular and continuous supply, then there is no problem for it, when it is short every, one tries to get sugar by any means gives commissions in order to make sugar stock for future consumption. This mad rush would naturally have impact on the law and order situation in the Society. Some relevant decisions should be taken by the society as to how sugar in future is to be distributed. This is a crucial function of society which is of a deep concern for its politics.[49]

And the members of the society must accept that decision as Authoritative and every one must consider the distribution as obligatory and binding. The implication is very clear. Those who challenge he will be punished or severely dealt with. Society uses force, coercion, so that people must obey its decisions by and large every one abides by the distribution on account of self-interest and also in the interests of the others. Thus, value allocations are regarded authoritative. Thus the goods and services are authoritatively distributed in families, clubs, business firms, associations and the like. David Easton said these are the para-political bodies or structures.[50]

Thus, Authoritative Allocation of values for the society is quite comprehensive concept. It is a ongoing and multi-dimensional process.[51] It involves power, authority, conflict, consensus and above all dynamics of Decision Making. When the decisions regarding the distribution of goods are taken, the decision makers are called upon to solve the various conflicting interest by developing consensus among them. Further decision-makers are called upon to solve the various conflicting interests by developing consensus among them. Further decision-makers symbolise the power and authority of society. They are required to employ force and coercion against those who refuse to abide by the allocations.

Above all, the decisions which is taken must be implemented or enforced, or executed. Thus, we find that value allocation is an area for more comprehensive than either power and conflict. It includes both power and conflict and many more things. Therefore, we can say that value allocation is the only single largest concern of politics. Public policy is the study of value allocation.

INPUT-OUTPUT STRUCTURES

For understanding the public policy in better terms we can refer to the Input-Output model given by G.A. Almond and Feed-back model given by David Easton. Political System is a set of interactions having structures, each part of which performs its functions in order to keep it like an on-going concern, it is also a set of processes routinely converting inputs into outputs. In systems technology and influence that affects the functioning of a political system is input. Inputs, in a political system, result in demands upon and support for the system, which converts them into outputs in the form of authoritative policies and implementing actions. Inputs originate in the environment of the system and within the system itself. Inputs originating within the system are sometimes called with-inputs. G.A. Almond has tended to classify inputs of political system into generic functional categories like political Socialization and recruitment, interest articulation, interest aggregation and political communication. Output activities are those which are carried on by a political system in response to demands or stresses placed upon the system in the form of inputs. Outputs usually take the form of governmental policies programmes, decisions and implementing actions.[52] They have been categorised as rule making, rule enforcing and rule interpreting functions carried on within a larger social system.[53] Political system is seem as a conversion process performing work, producing outputs, and altering its environment, with a continuous exchange between a political system and its environment based on the steady operation of the dynamic processes. At the same time, the approach provides numerous concepts for dealing both with political dynamics. In the form of systemic adaptation processes and even with purposive redirection in the form of goal-changing feed back with this perspective it is possible to deal with changes in the system itself, although the input-output approach focuses mainly on changes whose principal results are only to modify or streamline the system (young).

INPUT-OUTPUT MODEL

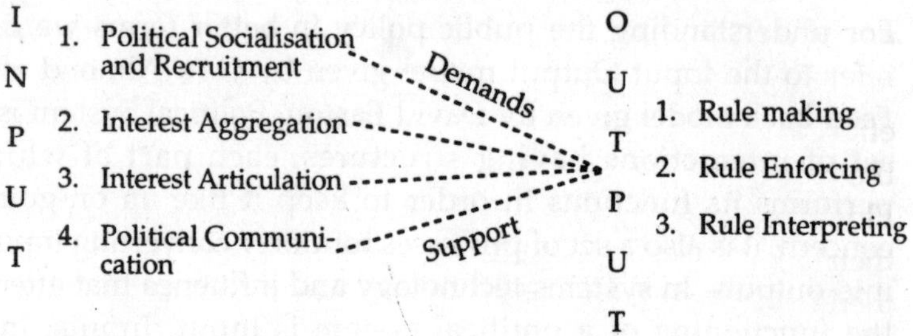

(A) Input Functions

The most outstanding contribution to the Input-Output thesis or approach comes from G.A. Almond. He developed seven functions scheme, and it consists of four input functions and three output functions. To him the input functions are the political functions and they are more important than the output functions. Output functions are the governmental functions.

Let us See the Input Functions

1. *Political Socialisation and Recruitment* : Prof. Almond and Verba have given the concept of political socialisation. Political socialisation is a process by which political cultures are maintained and changes.[53] Political socialisation is a psychological concept. The process of political socialisation is an ongoing process because political orientations, values and attitudes of the individuals continue to change. It is a natural process. It starts as soon as the child is born. But the process of political socialisation is not uniform throughout. Sometimes it is slow and sometimes particularly at the time of major crisis, it becomes very fast and quick. The process of political socialisation becomes so rapid and quick that the people change their approach in an overnight. For example, Jallianwala Bagh tragedy in 1919 resulted in the change of the attitudes of the Indians towards the British government very

rapidly. A quick political socialisation process is likely to disturb the society very rapidly and quickly, on the other hand, if the process of political socialisation is slow, then the whole political system might work smoothly.[54]

Briefly speaking the main elements of political socialisation are—

1. *The Role of Elders* : The authoritarion method is very effective, powerful and useful for socialisation. It starts with the parents. In this category fall parents, elders, teachers etc. Elders command respect from the child and children carryout their instructions. Since the fear of punishment is also there, therefore, the process of socialisation become easy and speedy. This is a temporary method and it disappear as soon as the influence of authority is over.

2. *The Role of Equals* : In society an individual comes across many persons who are equal to him in authority. He has understanding with them and usually learns co-operation, adjustment with them. Infact, there are many process which he learns from his equals eather than the elders.

3. *The Role of Education* : In modern society education becomes more important Educated person is respected everywhere. Now-a-days, education has taken over the responsibility of the family. The way he is taught has far-reaching consequences for the child in the process of socialisation.

4. *The Role of Environment* : The environment play a very important role in the process of socialisation. Those children who get healthy environments and surroundings soon get socialised and pickup good manners and habits compared with the children who do not get good environments. As a result of environment the criminals and offenders come out of the society. It is due to environments that one becomes either social or anti-social or conscious or unconscious.[55]

5. *Role of Friends* : It is said that a friend in need is a friend indeed.[56] An individual mixes with his friends. These friends have clashing and conflicting interests. It is through these

friends the process of socialisation speeds and he begin to love or hate political processes, systems and institutions.

6. *Role of Married Life* : But the married life gives a new outlook to the process of socialisation. After marriage both the husband and wife required to learn of interdependence and adjustment. They begin to love each other and appreciate the feelings of others in this regard. The attitudes of husband and wife towards politics either quicks or slowdown the process of socialisation.

Thus there are primary as well as secondary socialising influences. Among the primary structures the role of family, church, school, voluntary associations is significant. The secondary influences, namely, media of communications, political parties and governmental influences. Political socialisation is essential to the understanding of the other political functions.

There is a close relationship between Political socialisation and Political recruitment. Infact, on begins, where the other ends. Recruitment is actual induction into the system. Recruitment functions cannot be fully separated from the socialisation function. Recruitment into political roles may be based on universalistic or general criteria on the one hand or particularistic criteria on the other. The selection of office holders by lot, by election, by some proof of ability or performance, such are the examples of recruitment on the basis of universal criteria on the one hand, recruitment from a particular tribe or ethnic group is an example of particularistic criteria of recruitment on the other. Selection from the Royal or Aristocratic families is an example of particularistic criteria In primitive and the traditional recruitment to political systems was based on particularistic and hereditary criteria.[57] But in modern times ability and performance somehow taken into account in recruitment. In modern times particularistic criteria also enters in the matters of political recruitment. Thus the family relationships, social status, class, school ties and friendship enter into political recruitment in all modern political systems. But the styles of political recruitment vary from one system to another.

2. *Interest Articulation* : This is the second important input function. Interest articulation is the process by which individuals and groups make demands upon the political decision makers. Those demands may be (*a*) demands for allocation of goods and services, (*b*) demands for regulation of behaviour, (*c*) demands for participation in the political system, (*d*) demands for communication, (*e*) demands for formulation of specific policies. Demands and supports are vital for the survival of the political system. Supports are material supports paying taxes, military service etc. participatory supports—Participatory supports includes political discussion, respect for public authority, symbols, ceremonies. Further supports are classified as overt support—which is open, we all of us identify it. Covert support—which is manifest, we cannot see it. This type of support is coming from inside. Specific support—supports for a specific policy or issue. All out support—It is nothing but total support to the policies formulated by the party in power. Interest Articulation is identified with pressure groups. Interest articulation is a process of joining issues or making of common interests among all divided groups. Interest articulation maintains the boundary line between society and the political system.[58]

Articulation of interest can take place by and through many structures.

1. Institutional Interest Groups.
   Legislature, executive and armed forces.
2. Non-Institutional Interest Groups.
   Tribes, racial groups, priests, regional, religious and class groups.
3. Anomic Interest Groups.
   Demonstrations, strikes, riots and other violent means. They articulate their demands through physical force and vidence.

4. Associational Groups.
   Civil, cultural, and other commercial associations or trade unions.

3. *Interest Aggregation* : It is a process is which demands are combined in the form of alternative course of action.[59] Interest already articulated are combined, accommodated and compromised. Political parties involves in interest aggregation. Interest aggregation is identified with political party. Interest aggregation enables the system to operate in a simplified, acceptable, responsive and efficient manner. It becomes easy for it to jump from input to output stage. Aggregation makes it possible to act in a measurable and calculated way. However, the distinction between interest articulation and interest aggregation is subtle and flexible. Political parties are suitable to do the interest aggregation job. Political parties are supposed to be involved in the process of interest aggregation. They can be classified as.

1. Authoritarian Party System—Totalitarian party examples U.S.S.R. Italy, Germany, etc.
2. Non-Authoritarian party System—Nationalists Unit Movements.
3. Competitive Bi-Party System—Like those in U.S.A. and U.K.
4. Competitive Multi-Party System—Such as France, India.

4. *Political Communication* : Since all functions are performed by means of political communication, communication function is very crucial. Communication make or mar the system.[60] It is life blood of the political system. Communication is the medium or media through which all other functions are performed. Almond says that it is like a circulation of blood in human body communication is transmitted through symbols, languages. It's scope and form is wider than conventional terms—like public opinion, mass media, *i.e.*, Newspapers, TV, Radio, Magazines, Books, etc. It is a sharing of information and values by various means and expressions thereof. The legimate physical force takes the form of political

communication. It performs the function of boundary maintenance by deciding on the issues as political or non-political. Political communication connects society and polity directing. There is a need of media to make a free flow of information from society to polity but also from one political structure to another and also from political system to the environment. It transmits aggregated interests.

Though it is one of the seven functional requisites, yet it becomes a 'regulator of regulators' by disallowing the structures not to cross their boundaries.[61] Every form of non-political communication is forbidden by law. In open or democratic societies, communication to a large extent remains free. Its structures are multidimensional and neutral and their functioning is smooth, speedy, flexible and expanding. Open communication System strengthens inputs of the system towards equilibrium. Thus, no operation of the political system can take place unless the parts of the system can communicate to each other. All functions of the political system are performed by the means of communication. Political socialisation is imparted through communication. The demands which have been articulated and aggregated are communicated to the decision makers. Legislators, bureaucrats, Judges discharge their functions by communicating with one another and other parts of the political system. No social and political interaction is possible without communication.[62]

However, as a process, it can be studied and compared on the basis of Homogeneity, Mobility, Volume, Cost and Direction. It can also be related to levels of education, literacy, language, class, caste and values. In such analysis, role of interpreters, analysis, spokesmen and intellectuals cannot be neglected.

(B) OUTPUT FUNCTIONS

Political system is marked by two main forces—Inputs and Outputs. Input functions have been called as political functions. The output functions also have been designated as governmental functions. The Political system converts the inputs into outputs. Though output functions have been classified into three traditional manner yet, he separated them analytically from traditional structures—legislature, executive and judiciary. The three output functions are, Rule-making, Rule enforcing and Rule adjudication—are functions which can be performed by any formal or informal structures. They can be discussed in brief.

5. *Rule-Making* : It is highly normative and general function. Rules are formulated. The concept of 'Rule' is broader and wider than law. In ancient times the rule-making function was performed by some 'Godly' person, priest or saint. Religion and religious persons expanded it further. As the people have have faith in them, their divine origin and destination they accepted, followed and obeyed almost blindly.[63] Later kings and lords performed this function. With the rise of democracy—the specific structures like Legislature, Legislative Committees, Executive, higher bureaucracy began to perform this job *i.e.*, Rule-making by men. Rules are formulated by the Legislature. Rule-making too has two levels-Higher and Lower or ordinary.

At the higher level or governing level, there is superior law or constitution embodying the basic elements of values and culture. At the ordinary or lower level, the Lower House, which is directly elected by the people on the basis of adult franchise makes ordinary laws. All laws or rules actually represent human interests, which operate through political parties, pressure or interest groups, elite and other vested interests.

6. *Rule-Enforcing*: After making of rules or formal recognition of the will or interests of the people, the next category of functional requisites is 'Rule-Enforcing'. Rule-enforcing is nothing but rule execution, rule-implementation or rule application. Rule enforcing is nothing but putting of rules into actual practice.[64] In modern times, it is the biggest part of the Outputs. After the rules are formulated or framed, they are applied and exforced. It is a function performed by modern bureaucracies. Rule-application is done by the bureaucracy.

In the olden times or days most of these functions are performed by society or community and various religious bodies. Functions left with the political system were performed by Army or Aristocracy. Citizens or subjects themselves were responsible for many operations. Later on Rule-enforcing or application required specialised and expanded structures to deal with the situation. State's monopoly over coercive power appeared in the form of bureaucracy. Originally, it was a sub-structure, but later on, became on autonomous structure or system. Its functioning requires on independent study. To what extent it is carrying out the rules or wishes of the people in practice? Is it serving the purpose to which it was made and developed? Does it have its own interests and purposes to serve? Rules unless implemented faithfully can cause much frustration and decay in the system.

7. *Rule-Interpreting* : Rule interpreting is nothing but Rule-adjudication. It is a function performed by the Judiciary.[65] Rule application functions broadly apply rules. There are situations wherein it is difficult to apply or if applied, it can caused injustice or grave injury to some persons. Such difficult situations require specialised functioning by expert, experienced, intelligent, neutral and independent structures. Rule adjudication or Rule-enforcing is done by the courts. It is necessary that Rule-interpreting structures courts, Tribunals, popularly selected Judicial bodies etc.—remain free from the influences of other structures and are also able to do their job Well. Court resolves conflicting situations in society. Sometimes rules are violated, courts imposes penalty for its enforcement. Secret police are employed in totalitarian states to pursue individuals who violating a rule. Courts function is to keep structures and sub-structures within given confines and see that the system operates on expected lines. It is the job of Rule interpreting bodies to see that both inputs and outputs are operating in accordance with the basic rules formulated and accepted on the political system.[66]

However, functioning of Rule-interpreting itself is hypothetical and prove defective to equillibrium of the system on account of its in capacity, favouritism, inexperience, cast, delay, lengthy procedure and non-implementation of their decision.

FEED BACK MODEL

Another model through which the politics policy relationship is established in political system is the feedback model given by David Easton. It is also known as the Black-Box model. Easton has been mainly concerned with depicting the relationship between a system and the environment in which it is located. He has drawn the attention to the relationship between politics and other aspects of social life and postulates the existence of a close interaction between a system and environment. The prime components of his model pertaining to input are demands and support and decisions and policies as that of output (Easton 1953).

FEED BACK MODEL

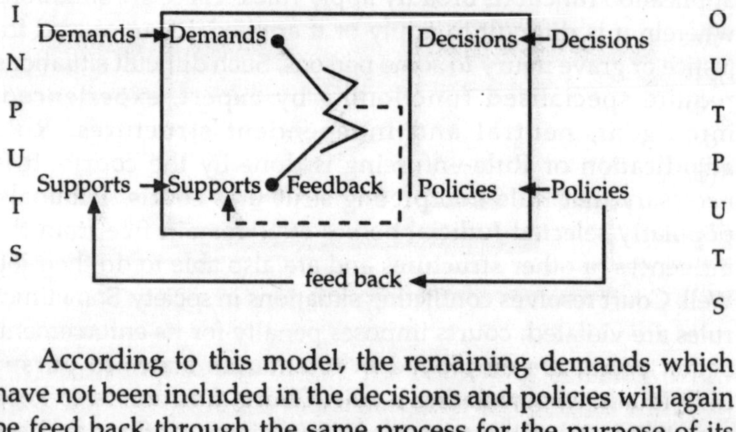

According to this model, the remaining demands which have not been included in the decisions and policies will again be feed back through the same process for the purpose of its conversion into decisions and policies. Let us suppose that the demand on a public policy 'B' consisting of three components B1, B2, B3 was made in order to get a policy or decision made on it. After putting through the process of conversion, the result or the output was that decision on B1 and B3 was taken but B2 was left out. Again through the feed back mechanism the component B2 would be fed for getting a decision made on it.

But at this time, the issues raised for not deciding about B2 would be throughly sorted out.[67]

The input-output model and the Feed-back model establish the relationship between politics and policies in a political system and also makes clear the role, taking into consideration both the internal and external factors, played by different agencies in arriving at certain decisions. As a concept in politics, policy has atleast two quite definite versions. On the one, often the policies are termed as the ways to do things, for example "It is the policy of this office to handle requests in such-and-such a way". In this sense policy would answer the questions. "How do you do things around here?" and may be called administrative policy. Alternatively, policies are often regarded as substantive programmes, referring specifically to the content of what is being done, and not necessarily to know it is being done. Policy in this sense answers the questions. "What do you do around here?" and "What kinds of problems do you handle." Studies of public policy often employ both meanings. How a programme is taken up, and what is the programme. The way a programme is administered affects its content and result. Still the two meanings should be kept district, since they refer to analytically separate things (Britannica Encyclopaedia).

BASIS OF POLICY FORMULATION

Broadly speaking there are four ways through which administration collect the necessary information.

1. *Internal Sources* : In every department we find the reports, returns, statements and various other materials. These reports and other material are recorded by the department for the future use whenever the need arises. Some departments employ special agencies for the collection of data in certain special fields. Several Ministries in India have established special machinery for the collection of statistics and data helps for policy making. The Central Statistical Organisation, The National Sample Survey, The Bureau of Public Enterprises and various other organisations are working for the collection of

information and statistics. The data so collected are property processed, organised and interpreted to reveal certain facts essential for policy making.[68]

2. *External Sources* : The internal source are not sufficient. The are only supplements. The administrator also collects the information from the external sources. He establishes contacts with private bodies, Unions, Associations, Chambers etc., in order to get true picture of facts. Internal informations are likely to be biased, they are inaccurate and unreliable because they travels through official channels. In our country government does consult the public opinion through various labour unions, chamber of commerce and other professionals associations before five year plans is actually approved, the draft prepared is thrown open for discussion to various bodies all over the country. The suggestions received are considered, incorporated and also approved in working out the final plan.[69]

3. *Special Investigations* : Special investigations are conducted by the appointment of the committee and commissions.[70] These Committees finds the facts in the particular matter or field. Such investigations are very useful for policy making. They provide maximum thought in particular field. Examples of such committees/commissions are many in our country and abroad. The Royal Commission appointed from time to time in England Hoover Commission in U.S.A., Central Pay Commission, University Grants Commission, Local Finance Enquiry Commission, the Administrative Reforms Commissions etc. are examples of special investigating bodies in India. These commissions examine the witnesses, both official unofficial obtain facts and views and which they convey to government in the farm of recommendations and these recommendations serves as a basis of policy making.

4. *Research and Survey* : Research and studies may be organised by the government or non-official agencies to discover certain facts and views. Administrative Research may be conducted by such bodies like O & M. It is in the cabinet secretariat.[71]

Similarly non-official bodies like Indian Institute of Public Administration (IIPA), New Delhi, British Institute of Public Administration (BIPA) also conducts research and provide facts for policy making. Technical research and study may be conducted by Technical Institutions. The Geological, Botanical, Zoological Surveys of India. Atomic Energy Commission, Oil and Natural Gas Commission etc., are some of the examples of institutions engaged in research.[72]

Dilemmas of Policy-Making Process in India

The policy makes process in India has run into many troubles and pitfalls. It has not been successful to the expectations of the Indians. Why it has not been successful? For this many reasons can be given and many factors are responsible. It has been receiving criticism and reactions from the public great scholars, eminent politicians and parliamentarians.[72]

The reason can be summed up as follows :

1. *Poor Implementation* : In India poor implementation is deeply affected by the local politics.[73] In India pressure groups are not so active at the stage of policy making and policy implementations. As a result, the implementation of socio-economic policies is ultimately determined by the local political interests and pressures. Policy remains frustrated and benefits goes to others other than target groups. Thus, in India, policy implementation is very weak and poor.

In India, we notice today that there is no timely enforcing of the plans, policies and programmes. The policies have not been able to reach their targets. The failure of policies are caused on account of natural calamities like floods, famines, and lack of resources. That is why it is said that "Indian are good planners, but bad doers."[74]

2. *Evils of Bureaucracy* : The governmental administration in India has been proved too weak, ineffective and inefficient as it cares more for the rules, regulations and formalities without caring the real needs, requirements and problems of the people. Corruption has become routine in governmental administration.[75] It cannot be eradicated either by law or by

an ordinance. Both citizens and the government are equally held responsible for the evils of corruption.

We talk of neat, clean, effective, impartial and efficient administration, but in practice, quite opposite or reverse is the result. So, the evils like red-tapism, nepotism and corruption etc. have become the hurdles or difficulties or impediments in the way of policy execution.

3. *Absence of Systematic Study and Research* : India had no arrangement or provision for systematic application of thought as to policy formulation and implementation. In India there is no organ for detailed inter-disciplinary study necessary for policy making.[76] Ad-hocism prevails in policy making process. Policy formulation in India is in an unsatisfactory state of affairs. The search for alternatives is an essential exercise in policy making provision at the earliest must be made in each department for enquiry and research before a policy is defined and put into operation. Research and enquiry should be carried out with the close co-operation of the administrative departments. Specialists should be appointed to such tasks. Senior officers in all departments must devote an adequate amount of time to enquire and research and keeps contacts with researchers which at present is negligible.

The policy advisory committee is attached to the cabinet secretariat consisting of Minister of State for External Affairs. Advisory Committee must also consists of Minister of State for Defence, Minister of State for External Security and some senior civil servants and experts. It's job is to formulate the current policies. The committee enjoys only advisory role. It does not meet regularly.

4. *Tenure System Under Stress* : Tenure system of the secretaries are under stress and strain, because they are sent on deputation's say for example five or six years. After the deputation period is over, they hesitate to go back to their parent departments. They are not ready to quit post and they make all kinds of efforts to prolong their tenure. Postings in the central secretariat are open to I.A.S. senior officer's

theoretically. But practically deputations are based on minister recommendations. Further, the opportunities for deputation have not been distributed equally. On return from secretariat the civil servants should be welcome to their states and field agencies and they must not be treated as punishment postings.[77]

5. *Departmentalism : A Hindrance to Policy Making* : Policy making suffers from another weakness, *i.e.,* departmentalism. Policies are formulated or made very narrowly *i.e.,* on departmental basis. Each department has its peculiar view points. They are narrowly oriented *i.e.,* narrow specialism. It hinders in formulating a unified policy. Indeed, departmentalism hinders sound policy making and implementation.[78]

Policy Analysis : Public policy analysis is concerned with governmental behaviour. Analysis is the basis of policy. What the government actually chooses to do or not to do forms the core of policy enquiry. Major policy decisions are taken by the government in such areas as defence, industry, agriculture, education and so on. Besides, financial expenditure, such decisions produce important and wide ranging consequences. These questions are now being raised by policy analysis. Policy making knowledge has wider concern. It deals with the system of policy making activity, how it operates and how it can be improved. Policies should be comprehensively examine the facts, bringout their implications and relationship between cause and effect between measures and their impact. In the absence of these studies policies may far.[79]

It is said that once the policies are formulated, their implementation has to be effectively started. We in India have framed or evolved several policies over the last fifty five years. Not all the policies have been successful. The policy of regulation of industry has not succeeded but on the other hand, led to black economy and misuse of industrial licensing. The policy for the increase in agricultural production has only partially succeeded. The policy of land reforms and co-operative forming has failed because of lack of capacity to implement the policy. The policies of Panchayati Raj or democratic decentralisation have not been successful because of lack of steady and long term political commitment. The science and technology policy, though based on the concept of self-reliance has led to a technological gap. The education policy has not succeeded either in elimination of illiteracy or improvement of the quality of education. There are so many areas where policy re-examination is called for.[80]

Assumptions Public Policy : Political Scientist Charles O. Jones makes a number of observations about public policy in general. Following are the nine important assumptions of public policy analysis :

1. Events in society are interpreted in different ways by different people at different times. This first assumption of Jones can be illustrated by considering the event. First, facts are disputed. The increase rates in crimes may be largely statistical. Interpretation of facts is also different. For this we need the more and better police protection. Government should improve the programmes for the elimination of poverty, slums and other conditions that cause people to commit many crimes.[81]

2. Many problems may result from the same event. It is the Jones' second important assumption about public policy analysis. Economic problem is the most important problem. If the economy of a nation is not sound tax yield decrease, services to the public are reduced. Pleasure travel and entertainment expenditures decline. Less expensive modes of transportation are preferred. These are some of the effect.

3. People have varying degree of access to the policy process in government. Financial resources, strength of organisation and political power are important factors in gaining such access. The government should make positive efforts to help the consumers, minorities and the poor. And what government should do is to reduce the influence of powerful group.[82]

4. Most problems are not solved government, though many are acted on it. The problems that the contemporary

government facing is intricate, complex and complicated. And there are no complete or permanent solutions to those problems. Government generally creates condition that permit private individuals and organisations to succeed in their work. Government do not have all the answers, solutions and remedies to these problems.[83]

5. Policy makers are not faced with a given problem. Jones' point is that policy makers are not usually presented with a defined problem. They must determine the cause of the difficulties before they can propose solutions. First, real problem should be solved. The real problem may be racial, caste discrimination, low income, urban disorganisation, alienation and similar factors.

6. Problems and demands are constantly being refined and redefined in the policy process and policy makers adjust their sights accordingly. Objective events can change the reality. Definition and re-definition is inherent in the policy process, because of the complexity of the problem.

7. Policy-makers sometimes define problems for people who have not defined problems for themselves. Sometimes policy makers may lack the time or analytical skill. They refuse to acknowledge the existing difficulties. There is a danger that the policy makers may make hasty erroneous. Superficial or arbitrary judgements in defining the problem. Safeguards should be provided into the policy making system to reduce this possibility.

8. Much policy is made without the problems ever having been clearly defined. Administrators were given broad authority in the act. But he is not sure what ought to be done. The fact is that broad legislation is to be passed, a new agency created, large sums appropriated ignoring the problems of poverty.[84]

9. All policy system have bias. The bias may be of different kinds. If the policy making is dominated by the very wealthy, the lower-middle classes which ever the most influential group, the policies will mostly reflect the interests of that group.

Decisions may be controlled by oligarchies or some persons may have much more influence than others. The policy making system have been constructed to provide numerous checks and balances as in the United States System.[85]

TYPES OF PUBLIC POLICY

Public policies are expected to be so much multifarious in character and kinds whereby each and every area connected with the lines of the individuals, both within the country and outside the country, is touched and fairly covered. Alongwith it the policies are also to be made whereby the stance of the government towards foreign powers has to be kept in view. The concept of city state, as it used to be in ancient times, is no more in existence.[86] The place of city states has been taken by the National States and the growing awareness, highly developed technology and the desire to be more advanced are the factors which amount to the emergence of various types of policies whereby the demands of the masses and the foreign and defence policies of the nation become clear.

Policies are of various types. They could be classified as under.

1. *Substantive* : These are concrete policies which take into account the general welfare and development of the society.[87] It deals with the society as a whole and not with any particular or privileged segments of it. It deals with economic stabilization, education and employment opportunities to all irrespective of caste, colour, sex or creed, measures of safety law and order enforcement, pollution and adulteration eradication etc. In broader and wider terms these policies deal with the stable society living of the inhabitants in a given political system. Since substantive policies have vast areas of operation, therefore, the governmental agencies have to formulate these by thoroughly analysing various problems attached with such kind of policies. For example, if the law and order enforcement or execution policy has to be framed then the government has to specify the circumstances under which the police or para-military forces would be acting in a drastic

manner to provide peace and stability, because we are not living now in the police state but are in the welfare state, so that policy has to be formulated keeping the prime character of the constitution in view.

For enacting policy, for providing economic stabilization the government has to be effectively deal with the issues like : how to maximise the scarce sources and make their consumption effective, how to keep out-put of abundant resources to the required level of moral claims of economy etc. policy of education will deal with two aspects—moral and material. Moral objective is to ensure overall development of the personality and the development of scientific attitude among the citizen. Materialistic objective is to help them to be able to earn their both ends meet.

2. *Regulatory* : One of the most visible types of public policy is regulatory. Regulatory policies are those whereby the trade, business, safety measures, public utilities etc. are regulated by independent organisations having legal personality. These corporations and organisations work on behalf of the government. The regulatory policies provide large measures of administrative and financial autonomy to these organisations. The various examples of such organisations or corporations in India are : Life Insurance Corporation, Reserve Bank of India, Hindustan Steel etc. as Central Government undertakings, State Electricity Boards, State Transport Corporations, State Financial Corporations at State Government level, Damodar Valley Project, Bhakra Nangal Project under the joint management of Central and State governments.[88]

There are so many others of these kinds of corporations and organisations which are regulating the Railways, Air Lines, Shipping, Public Utility Services like water, gas, electricity etc. The Policies made by the government pertaining to these services and organisations rendering these services are known as regulatory policies. Regulatory policies are regulated through criminal law and statutes. They are regulated through the actions of Independent Regulatory Commissions. The food and drug administration, commerce commission are charged with the regulation of trade rates, businesses etc.

3. *Distributive* : Distributive public policies includes all public assistance and welfare programmes to society.[89] These differ from the substantive policies as those are for whole of the Society. But the distributive policies are meant for specific segments of society. These deals with grant of goods, public welfare and health services. These include policies like sterilization for family planning purposes, vaccination of children, adult education, flood relief, social insurance, mid-day meals to the school going children etc.

Distributive policies grant goods and services to specific segments of the population. One of the most prominent areas of distributive policies is health and welfare. All public assistance programmes are distributive.

4. *Redistributive* : The prime motive of the Redistributive policies is to rearrange the basic programmes of social and economic gains. In other words, Redistributive policies aim at rearranging one or more of the basic schedule of social and economic rewards.[90] They take more money from the rich than from the poor. The rescheduling with the enactment of public policies is made in such a manner whereby the rich have to pay more as taxes in comparison to the poor. Certain public goods and welfare services are in proportionately divided among certain segments of society by the distributive policies, the amendments to the proper effect of such distributive policies is also made through the enactment of Redistributive Policies. Progressive policies are the good example of redistributive policies.

5. *Capitalization* : Capitalization policies are different in nature than the substantive, regulatory, distributive and redistributive policies. No welfare and provisions of public goods in made through capitalization policies as is done through other types of public policies. Under the capitalization policies, financial subsidies are given by the Union Government to the state and local governments and also to the

central and state business undertakings[91]. Sometimes, subsidies, pertaining to some other important spheres are also given by the Union government. Policies regulating such live issues are known as capitalization public policies.

Capitalization policies include :

1. Cash payments to farmers (For example, sugar beet and cane growers to improve the farm industry),
2. Tax subsidies to encourage exploration and production in selected industries,
3. Credit Subsidies. For example, low interest loans are given to Municipalities.

6. *Ethical* : In the moral and ethical values, the citizens play a significant and prominent role in shaping the destiny of the nation.[92] It is not the gold and silver which make the country great but it is always the human brings which establish the greatness of their country by virtue of certain ethical and moral principles.[93] There are certain public policies which bring forth the adequate norms for some ethical and moral issues. Ethical public policy has a separate category from other regulative policies of Law and Commerce. It is a well known fact that corruption is rampant and widespread in these days and it would not be wrong to say that it is at its peak now. The major reasons for it are lack of effective public opinion, improper education and less awareness among the masses. Economic measures to improve the general lot, enforcement of professional code of ethics and propagation of new social value among the public by the government led to the enactment of public policy formulating preventive Measures of Corruption Act.

7. *Ideological* : The ideological policies flow from the very basic character of the government itself or from the fundamental constitution of the country. Capitalism, Socialism, Marxism, Secularism, Liberalism, Conservation, Fascism and Nazism are the ideological policies. Ideological policies were prevalent in those days such as that of Adam Smith, the author of the 'Wealth of Nations', acknowledged and accepted as the

first systematic and scientific treatise on Economic.[94] The basic policy of the laissez faire and the maxim, "That government is best which governs the least"; and this policy is related to planning and social ownership of the means of production are highly ideological in nature.

8. *Macro Economic* : This policy is more technological rather than ideological in nature. It has many dimensions. Thus, macro-economic policies cover such important items such as price and income policy, fiscal policy, banking policy, wage policy and policies to regulate and promote production.

9. *Development Policies* : This is a general policy and is more technological in nature.[95] It has also many dimensions—social, political, economic, educational and cultural. Development policies may cover the entire gamut of policies to promote savings and investment, built-up public sector enterprises, develop human resources and create a sense of motivation and achievement in the people.

10. *Sectoral* : Then there are sectoral policies. Such as the foreign policy, agricultural policy, food policy, industrial policy, food policy, science and technology policy. Then there are inter-sectoral policies. Sectoral policies have inter-sectoral implication.[96] Sectoral policies and inter-sectoral policies are inter-related. Thus, the defence policy is not just a question of policy for Army, Navy and Airforce. The defence policy is linked up with the domestic, economic and industrial policy and the foreign policy. If the domestic economy is strong it can support a big defence effort. On the other hand, if the domestic economy is weak, a strong defence has to be ruled out. Similarly, foreign policy creates friends rather than enemies. The defence policy itself would assume different dimensions.

11. *Original* : These policies are defined by the constitution, the laws of the land or the legislature or cabinet. These are all the highest policy maining bodies or authorities. These policies are broad in scope.

12. *Appeal* : These policies move or flows through the appeal made by the subordinates to their superiors.[97] This

policy establish the links or relationship between the superior and the subordinates. These policies are in the form of appeal made by the Subordinate to the superior officers. How the matter should be handled the subordinate may appeal to his superior.[98]

13. *Implied* : These policies develop where no clear policy exists. In such cases the executive officers adopt their own guidelines. They take into consideration the spirit of the original policies.[99]

14. *Externally Imposed Policies* : Political parties at the time of electron declare their policies through election magnifestos. The party which comes in power influences the government to implement these policies. Similarly, the opposition parties also influence the policies by pointing out its defects or deficiencies or shortcomings and compel the government to reformulate the policy. Sometimes pressure groups and strong labour unions exerts their influence on the government or the legislature.[100]

REFERENCES

1. Strauss, Leo, What is Political Philosophy? Glencoe, Ill : Free Press, 1959.

   Public Policy is emerging as an inter-disciplinary subject and as such it is related to other social sciences.
2. Organisations decisions are made within the framework of the public policy.
3. Connolly, William, The terms of Political Discourse, Lexington, 1974. Public Policies are prior to any action.
4. Easton David, The Political System, New York, 1953.
5. Frohock, Fred M., "Notes on the Concept of Politics", The Journal of Politics, May 1974.
6. In the past the states were called as police states and their duty was the maintenance of law and order and they were least bothered about the welfare of the people. Such states were called to perform the negative functions. But modern states are the welfare states and their duties and functions are widening and broadening day by day. Modern States perform the positive functions and their role is constructive ones.

7. Providing public facilities like health, education, electricity, roads are the main priorities of modern states.
8. Frohock, Fred M., Public Policy-Scope and Logic, London Prentice Hall, 1979.
9. For example, Aristotle made the comparative study of the states. He studied 169 states, or political systems before classifying them.
10. Aristotle said that no form of government is stable. Governments always moved in circle.
11. This is the idea derived from the Machiavelli's prince.
12. Schelling, Thomas, The Strategy of Conflict, New York, Oxford University Press, 1963.
13. In despotism, a Monarch protect and promote his self interests. He becomes selfish. Power is utilised and misused for securing selfish ends.
14. Brams, Steve, Game Theory and Politics, New York, Free Press, 1975.

    The various organs of the governments are inter-related and inter-connected.
15. According to Austin citizens or subjects must obey the sovereign without questioning or challenging.
16. Will not force is the basis of the state said T.H. Green.
17. These ideas are taken from the Communist Manifesto of Karl Marx.
18. Von Neumann, J. and Oskare Morgenstern, Theories of Games and Economic Behaviour, New York, John Willey, 1964.
19. Even non-governmental agencies also play an important role in the formulation of public policies.
20. Salisbury, Robert, "The Analysis of Public Policy : A Search for theories and Roles", in Political Science and Public Policy, ed : Austin Ranney, Chicago, Markham, 1968.
21. Aristotle, Politics, Translation of Rackham, London, Heinemann, 1932.
22. Miccoy, Charles N.R., The Structure of Political Thought, London, Mc-Graw Hill, 1963.
23. Policy making is an important part of the political system.

24. According R.E., Stone public policy is closely related to the government units and its environment.
25. Basil, Blackwell, Cocke : The Second Treatise of Government, Northwick, Fletcher and Son, 1976.
26. Public policy and the organs of the government are closely related.
27. Sabine, G.H., and Thorson, T.L., A History of Political Thought, Tokyo, Hott Saunders, 1963.
28. Public policies are related to the goals and not to the structures.
29. Rose, Dichard, Policy Making in Great Britain, London, Macmillan, 1969.
30. Sabine, G.H. and Thorson, T.L., A History of Political Thought, Tokyo, Holl Saunders, 1963.
31. The implementation are of public policy is very vast and wide and it covers a number of ramifications.
32. Dorothy, Fosdick, What is liberty? A Study in Political Theory, New York, 1939, p. 40-42.
33. *Ibid., op. cit.*, pp. 44-48.
34. The Policy implementation work is undertaken at all the levels. Those are Central, State and Local level.
35. Policy objectives are determined by various factors, pulls and pressures.
36. Feur, Lewis S., The Political Theory of Thomas Hill Green, New York, 1939.
37. Feur, Lewis S., Marx and Engles : Basic Writings on Politics and Philosophy, New York, Anchor Book, 1959.
38. Almond Gabriel A. and Powell, G.B., Comparative Politics : A Developmental Approach, Massachusetts, Little Brown and Company, 1975.
39. Eyestone, Robert, The Threads of Public Policy : A Study in Policy Leadership, Indiana Polis, Bobbs-Merrill, 1971.
40. Dye, Thomas R. Understanding Public Policy, Englewood Cliffs, Prentice Hall, 1975.
41. This definition is found in the Morgenthau's great book known as 'Politics Among the Nations.'
42. In the past politics was the study of the state and government. Its study of area was narrow and limited.

43. Politics is a double game-helping the well-wishers, friends and supports and denying facilities to ones enemies.
44. Politics as a game of 'how to acquire power, retain power, and expand or enlarge power.'
45. This definition is derived from the book 'A Framework of Political System' written by David Easton.
46. Anderson, James E., Public Policy Making, New York, Holt, Rinehart and Winston, 1979.
47. To David Easton, 'Allocation' means distribution.
48. Here David Easton used the term values in a economic sense. Values means goods and services.
49. *Ibid.*, David Easton, *op. cit.*
50. It is obligatory on the part of the individuals to obey the political system and those who disobey must be punished—David Easton.
51. Politics covers or involves the study of conflict, consensus, power, public policy, decision-making etc.
52. S.N. Eisenstadt, The Political Systems of Empire (New York : The Free Press of Glencoe, 1962), Chap. 1, p. 13.
53. Eisenstadt, Political Systems, *op. cit.*, Chap. 13.
54. For a more complete discussion of this process see Gabriel A. Almond and Sidney Verba, The Civic Culture (Princeton University Press, 1963), chap. 15.
55. Environment plays a very important role in mans life. In a good environment man cultivates good habits and in a bad environment, bad habits. It is the environment which can make or mar the man.
56. This is a English proverb and it actually applies to real friends.
57. David Apter, The Politics of Modernisation (Chicago : University of Chicago Press, 1965).
58. F.W. Riggs, The Ecology of Public Administration, (New Delhi : I.I.P.A., 1961).
59. Interest aggregation may be performed within all the sub-systems of the political system. It is done by the political parties.
60. David Easton, A System Analysis of Political Life (New York : John Wiley and Sons, Inc., 1965), p. 161.

61. Arthur Schlesinger, Jr., The Coming of the New Deal (Boston : Houghton Mifflin Company, 1959), especially pp. 521 ff.
62. Kenneth Boulding, The Image (Ann Arbor : University of Michigan Press, 1956), p. 101.
63. The divine origin theory was prevailed in the past as such people obeyed the kings blindly. Disobedience to king means disobedience to God such a faith was there in the ancient days.
64. See Ole Holsti, "The 1914 Case," The American Political Science Review, June, 1965, pp. 365-378.
65. See Lucy Mair, Primitive Government (Baltimore Penguin Books, Inc., 1962), pp. 35 ff.
66. Rule-interpreting bodies keeps the inputs and outputs in balance.
67. Barrington Moore, Jr., Terror and Progress U.S.S.R. Combridge, Harvard University Press, 1954, pp. 176ff.
67. *Ibid., op. cit.*, pp. 180ff.
68. Internal Sources are very essential for policy formulation.
69. Adamson Hoebel, The Law of Primitive Man (Cambridge : Harvard University Press, 1954, pp. 67ff.
70. Mukherji, N.K., 'Policy Making in India' The Indian Express, 5 December, 1985.
71. F.M.G., 'Policy Making and the Policy-Makers' in Richard Rose (ed.), Free Press, New York, 1969, pp. 355-68.
72. *Ibid., op. cit.*, pp. 368-375.
73. Ministry of Reconstruction, Report of the Machinery of Government Committee, Cd. 2230, London, HMSO, 1918, p. 6.
74. This is the idea taken from the book P.R. Krishna Aiyar, Public Administration', pp. 65-68.
75. Corruption is compared to a cancer as cancer paralyses every organ of the body.
76. The Hindustan Times, 26 August, 1983.
77. Reports on the Re-organisation of the Central Government, 1945-46, p. 27.
78. The Statesman, 27 April, 1986.
79. With the thorough investigation of the facts and figures, policy study fails.

80. A.R.C. Reports-Machinery of Government of India and procedures of its work, Vol. I, Part II, 1968.
81. Poverty is the main cause for all the ills, evils and the crimes.
82. A.R.C. Reports *Ibid., op. cit.*, Vol. II, Part III, 1969.
83. Problems of the society are not solved by the government alone, the private individuals, societies and organisations co-operation is required.
84. We cannot improve the administration without eliminating poverty. In India more than 40% of the people are living below the poverty line.
85. The Hindustan Times, 26 August, 1983.
86. The Hindu, 25 April, 2004.
87. The Deccan Herald, 24 March, 2002.
88. The Times of India, 20 January, 2004.
89. Barnard, Chester : The Functions of the Executive, Cambridge, Mass, Harvard University Press, 1938, pp. 44.
90. Chester, *Ibid., op. cit.*, 1939, pp. 47.
91. Chester, *Ibid., op. cit.*, 1940, pp. 48-50.
92. Moral issues are more important in building the image of the nation.
93. Barnard Chester, *op. cit.*, 1940, pp. 60-64.
94. Adam Smith a great economist, the author of the 'Wealth of Nations'.
95. Times of India, 14 Feb., 1958.
96. S.R. Maheshwari, Political Control Over Executive Departments in India, Philippine Journal of Public Administration, Vol. XXIV, No. 2, April 1980, p. 161.
97. G.A. Campbell, The Civil Service in Britain, London, Gerald Duchworth, 1964, p. 224.
98. Paul H. Appleby, Policy and Administration, Alabama, University of Alabama Press, 1949, p. 72.
99. Herbert Morrison, Government and Parliament, London, Oxford University Press, 1964, p. 332.
100. Labour organisations or the Unions exert their influence or pressure on the government for the fulfilment of their demands.

2

APPROACHES AND MODELS OF PUBLIC POLICY

The study of politics has fluctuated between two poles ever since men began to think about the nature of the polity. At one end were those who focused on the political institutions as key agencies of social control and social change. They regarded the behaviour of the state, and the intentions of the prince as the most important aspects. Conversely, others stressed how much extra political factors or conditions affected political events and institutions. Political System is the persisting pattern of human relationships through which authoritative decisions are made and carried out for a society.[1] A political system is distinguished from the other social systems by four characteristics—it is universal in its reach, extending to all members of a society, it claims ultimate control over the use of physical coercion, its light to make binding decisions is accepted as legitimate, and its decisions are authoritative, bearing the force of legitimacy and a substantial probability of compliance.

Within sub societal groups, like family, church, labour union or business organisation, the group decision making structure is regarded as political system. Whether one likes or not, a person is not at all beyond the reach of some kind of political system or the other. Politics is unavoidable fact of human existence and plays quite a substantial part in the lives of the individuals.[2] Politics is inescapable and so are its consequences. Policies plays a significant role in shaping and re-shaping the lives of the people in a given political structure. The policy analysis is equally important as it amounts to understanding of the environment around and to decide intelligently the best of the alternatives out of the available choices.

We know that the political scientists have not reached to a point of agreements on the kinds of policies to be formulated by the governments.[3] The term public policy has been defined in various ways by different authors. A simple definition of the policy states that "it is the important missions of government." The meaning of the words "important" and "missions" has been left unspecified. It also does not clarify the manner in which the policies are to be viewed. For example, regarding the problem of viewing government expenditure, an economist may focus on the allocation of funds to activities, such an economic stabilization, resource allocation, and income redistribution.

Components

The following components of the policies have been described. It will help us to understand the policy analysis.

1. A particular object or set of objects—Some designated part of the environment that is to be affected.
2. A desired course of events—a specific event of behaviour in the particular objects.
3. A selected line of action—a particular set of action chosen to bring about the desired course of events, not merely whatever the society happens to be doing towards the set of objects at the moment, but a deliberate selection one line of action from among several possible lines.
4. A declaration of intent—Some statement by the policy makers, whether broadcast publicly to all who will listen, or communicated secretly to a special few, on what they intend to do, how and why.

5. An implementation of intent—the actions actually undertaken *vis-a-vis* the particular set of objects in pursuance of the choices and declaration.

Issues in Policy Analysis : Some policy analysts broaden the term policy to include the effects that government actions have upon the people they are to serve. Some of these affects are encircled by the terms outputs, outcomes, or impacts of policy. A distinction to this effect between output (what government does) and outcome (what consequences follow from the outputs) has been made (Easton, 1965). Some others refer the term policy to mean broadly interdated decisions of the government. Whatever the case may be, public policy continues to be the focal point of politics in political system. Both the rulers and the ruled make the investment of their political resources to ascertain changes in the policy or to maintain the *status quo*. The queries made about the policy choices are : whether policy 'A' is good or bad and in which ways? What would be its cost? How many will get benefit of this? What would be the role of money? etc. Policy specialists have given five basic issues about public policy.

1. *What Choices are made and Why* : Studies of public policy are interested not only in what policy choices were adopted, that is, in the content of policy, but also in why one policy was adopted and not another. We know that the making of public policy involves choices among alternatives.[4] One often gets interested and anxious to know the specific reasons for the selection of a particular choice of an alternative.

2. *What are the Benefits and Losses* : The second issue in the policy analysis is the gains and losses of the policy *vis-a-vis* the public, *i.e.*, the common masses. On the basis of the demands or on the basis of some programme, the governmental actors made a selection of a particular alternative for making policy on that. An analysis of the policy can be made by looking at it from the angle of its positive and negative points and the benefits going to the people with its formulation, if so it how much percentage of the society, and similarly the losses suffered by how many in a given system.

3. *What Difference does Money Make* : Of course, which so ever policy would be formulated it will certainly have the involvement of funds. Let us suppose that the government has three priority areas Defence, Education, Social Welfare and on the government proposes to spend 50% of its total budget on these three areas and if out of that 50%, 40% is spent on the Defence, only then it would mean that the government has not done Justice to the other two areas of priority it had fixed up. A policy or set of policies can be analysed easily on the account of sum of amount being spent on it and keeping in view the other fields having equal importance for the formulation of policies and the money the government has for those.[5]

4. *What is the Impact of Public Policy* : The policies made by the government are expected to be practical and not theoretical or ornamental.[6] The exact worth of the policy can be measured by looking at the impact of the policy. Impacts represent the effects that a policy has on the target population and on other features of environment. Impacts may be intended or not. Some impacts are planned and anticipated by policy makers. Others, known as skill over effects represent the unanticipated products of policy unintended impacts arise because the political system consists of interrelated parts that influence one another and because detailed information about all the potential effects of a policy is unavailable. An elusive hope of policy formulators is to design public policies whose major consequences are intended and whose unintended impacts are either minimal or benign.

There may be no question for the policy maker that is more important than the policy impact. Policies may not accomplish the intended impacts. Skillover effects may be negative and reduce the systems capacity to attain other goals, and they may be problematic at best. Because research on policy impacts has been limited, the information available to decision makers is scarce. Public policy is partially made in the dark and biased on insufficient information about probable impacts on the environment.[7]

5. *The Fifth Issue in Policy Analysis is Evaluation* : How shall policies be evaluated. It is the most unavoidable and indispensable issue. Policies can be evaluated in terms of two major issues. Are the goals pursued by the policy desirable social ends? Do the policies actually accomplish the stated goals? If one dissents from the goals astensibly furthered by a policy, the issue the simple. Matters are usually more complex, however, because most policies are advocated in terms of seemingly consensual and even mobile goals. Policies are said to eliminate poverty, improve consumer choice, provide jobs, improve opportunities, and so on. The touch question is usually, therefore, whether the policy actually accomplishes its goal, and whether it attains the goal more effectively and at less cost than would alternative policies. Increasingly policy evaluation depends upon measurement. The rising status of precise measurement and quantitative analysis is evident, not only in academic studies of the causes and implications of certain policies-what might be called basic research-but also in applied studies that attempt to measure various cost benefit ratios of public policies.[8]

Approaches of Public Policy : Equality and action are the broad concerns of public policy and public policy is approached from different angles. They are :

1. Treat the question of purpose as unresolved. The study of public policy is basically concerned with the range of human needs and the political institution created to meet them. Yet there is no agreed and adequate definition of need, and much confusion prevails about the distinction between need preference and political problems. Moreover, the institutional arrangements meeting these needs through policies seem infinitely varied and have rapid rate of adsolescene. What is accepted in one decade as truth may be challenged in another. In analysing a policy an attempt has to be made to trace its uncertain objectives in a systematic manner public policy sometimes has multiple, conflicting and ambiguous objectives. The effort to clarify the aims of public policy and the way in which conflicting objectives are reconciled by those who

implement it is a useful method of formulating good questions about plans for the future. Further, policy is after all partly a redefinition of either political objectives or the constraints which inhibit the implementation of objectives already held. Because this is so, it follows that it must be difficult to discover what the governmental institutions are trying to attain, and whether its present arrangements facilitate the accomplishment of these evolving goals. The goals as given should not be accepted, it is necessary to scrutinize in light of inputs and outputs and outcoes.[9]

2. Attend to Practice As Well As Policy. One way of coping with ambivalents purposes is through vagueness and ambiguity. On analysing the purposes of legislation, we normally find that the political and ideological objectives, the goals of public policy, are open to many interpretations.[10] Ambiguity seems to be essential for agreement. When the purposes of policy are unclear and incompatible, each successive stage in the process of implementation provides a new context in which further clarification is sought. One of the consequences of passing ambiguous and inconsistent legislation is to shift the arena of decision to a lower level. The lack of consensus is resolved at the level of every day practice, through the concrete actions taken by administrators and practitioners. Hence, an analysis of practice must be combined with the study of policy. Indeed, the goals of programmes can often be understood best not from formal statements of legislature intent, but from every day practice. So programmes that appear different may be similar, while programmes that are similarly structured or intended may actually differ in their consequences.

3. Examine Policy in Historical Perspective. Public policies are formulated and implemented in a system which has its own environment and culture.[11] The formulators always make the policies which in one way or the other exhibit their keenness to resolve a issue and to satisfy the increasing demands of the public to that effect. The examination of a policy in historical perspective definitely amounts to possible results or outcomes the policy will have. Let us suppose that a policy was

formulated 20 years ago and people had reacted to it very sharply, again if policy somewhat similar to that will be formulated or has been enacted, it is going to meet the fate almost skin to the one met 20 years ago. An example to this can be the family planning policy implemented by the Congress (I) before January 1977 and after 1980, when the party came to power again after remaining out of it for three years.[12]

MODELS OF PUBLIC POLICY

Political Science has always resorted to metaphors, to the device of proceeding from the known to the unknown. Those who criticise the use of models need to understand that they too must use them. Models are essential part of policy analysis. Models are also called as paradigms.

Following are some of the prominent models of public policy :

1. *Rational Model.* The basic assumption in the rational model is that policy makers are rational. While making policies they go about in a sequential, logical manner, which means listing of objectives and their likely consequences. The objectives of the policies are listed and ranked them in their order of priority and all possible responses which should meet those objectives are considered, then all possible likely consequences connected and also responses are examined. This is actually an ideal approach to policy making. A policy is rational when it is most efficient. In calculating efficiency, all social, political and economic values achieved or sacrificed by a public policy have to be considered. Maximisation of 'net value achievement' is thus the hallmark of a rational policy.[13] Net value achievement means that in framing a policy all relevant values should be explicitly taken into account.

Firstly, in the rational model, the policy makers themselves are ignorant. They do not have the right values, they do not have knowledge. So, the assumption that the policy makers are rational. But most of the time neither the policy makers have knowledge nor do they have the skills to formulate these policies. They may not have the right values to lead the right policy response.

The second is organisational. The policies are made in departments, in Ministries. Therefore, there is departmentalism, the organisational culture which heavily determines the policy responses. So, the organisational limitation is also there.

The third is resources. It is physically impossible to list out all the responses, all the possible ways of talking the situation, because that is not only time consuming but it requires tremendous resources. In the context in which policies are made, there are not enough resources at governments disposal, even remotely to carry out such a process.[14]

Finally, there is the situational limitation, which means the policy makers do not start on a blank state. They are guided by existing procedures, they are hemmed in by precedents. Infact, the operation of past policies creates its own vested interests. Therefore, you do not start on a blank state, you do not start afresh, you are hemmed in by the past policies, by precedents. For all these reasons, it is felt that the rational model is merely an ideal which can never be reflective of what happens in reality.

Pre-requisites of rational policy-making are many. Firstly, an adequate understanding of social values is extremely important. Secondly, data and information regarding the alternative courses of action must be readily available. Thirdly, there must be a definite decision-making system in the organisation with adequate capacity to identify relevant data, analyse them property and predict the consequences of alternative courses of action.

2. *Incremental Model* : As opposed to this, is the incremental model which was put forward by Charles Lindblom which states the very opposite, that policies change in small incremental steps, may be two steps forward and one step backward or may be one step forward and two steps backwards. The policy makers do not go in for big huge

structural changes, or even analysis before undertaking policies.

There are certain characteristics of incremental policies. Firstly, they are status quo-oriented. Policies do not shift very greatly from the status. Secondly, they are reactive, in a sense, the policy makers cope with the problems as they arise, rather than anticipating them. There is no long term view or long term vision. The problems arise and you respond to them. It is purely responding to an unmediate need. Policies are often simply reaction to problems as they arise, without looking into long term consequences. Thirdly, incremental policies are means oriented.[15] What means you should have at your command. It means basically, that policies are made looking into what is your budgetary allocation, what is the staff at your disposal etc. You first pur forward the objectives and then see what kind of resources, what kind of technology or organisation you require to fulfil those objectives. Finally, incremental policies are by and large fragmentary. In the sense they do not see the policy arena as an integrated whole, rather, they see it in segments. This is true of most policies. Take the industrial policy. There is a separate policy for the small scale sector, a separate policy for large industries and a third policy for medium industries.

Similarly, if you take, the textile policy, there are separate policies for handlooms, power looms and mills. So, the policy approach is fragmentary. It is not unified or holistic, which means that policies are made on a sectoral basis without seeing their impaction other sectors. It obviously limits their utility. Thus, by and large, the policies are incremental.

3. *Descriptive Model* : There are descriptive models. Descriptive models are those which describe the situation. You can model an economy. This is usually in economic models, the model of economy in various sectors. An example of descriptive model is fore-casting. It is purely descriptive. It merely forecasts. It does not tell what to do. It just tell you what it will become. It is simply a forecasting model. If your money is in fixed deposit, what it will become in ten years. It is a

simple equation, which will tell you what is the total amount of your money at the end of ten years.[16] It does not tell you anything on whether you should take it out or put somewhere.

4. *Normative Model* : Normative model are much more complex. They not only prescribe and predict, but they also tell you the preferred alternative.

5. *Deterministic Model* : Deterministic models are those where the outcomes are certain, where you known exactly what happens, for example, the money in your bank deposit. The outcome is absolutely certain, it may double in five years or whatever, depending on the rate of interest.

6. *Probabilistic Model* : Probabilistic models are those where there is a large amount of uncertainty, there is a probability, the analysis gives you the trends, the outcome, then it will tell you what is the chance that such a thing will happen, whether 20 per cent, 30 or 40 per cent will be achieved. These are the differences. In one case, the outcome is not absolutely certain. It takes into account the uncertainty of the situation.

7. *Verbal Model* : There are also the verbal models which do not use mathematics. They are purely specified in symbolic terms. There is no mathematics. There is only simple logic. It just ranks the various objectives in terms of their importance. Of course, quantitative models are those which are heavily oriented towards mathematics.

8. *Institutional Model* : Policy as an institutional activity. Public policies are those which are developed by governmental actors and agencies. Public policy has a very thick relationship with the governmental bodies or officials.[17] Whether we view it from the formalism point of view of the governmental institutions or realism point of consideration, we come to the conclusion that a policy is not termed as a public policy unless it is formulated, implemented and enforced in true spirits by the various government institutions. Of course, the realistic approach has provided deep insight to the behaviour of the persons or institutions involved in the policy making process. Policies formulated by the government institutions are the ones

which are considered and regarded legal and legitimate.[18] These are the ones which have legal sanction behind them and it is compulsory and obligatory on the part of the citizens to obey and follow the policies formulated and enforced by the governmental institutions. Moreover, public policies made by the government are universal in nature and do cover all the segments of the society. A query can be raised to this effect that there are some policies which cover only specific segments of the society such as policy on adult education benefiting only the adults or policy on child welfare covering small children only. It may be added that even such type of policy will also be for all the adults or for all the children and not for any particular kinds. The government has been power and authority to get a policy formulated by it in complete form. No one can go against the actions of the government based on legitimation.

Institutionalism has a deep bearing on public policies because the policies are formulated and implemented through various institutions of the government. Institutionalism can be usefully put to use for policy analysis. There is a feeling that when the institutions and public policies have that great interrelationship then if the institutional structure changes would the public policies also change. We should not forget that the institutional structure and public policies are within a given environment having a culture of its own and certain traditions and values. So far the environmental factors do not change, the public policies would not undergo any considerable change.

9. *Elite Model* : Policy as Elite preference. Elite theory or model is a body of thought aimed at explaining the nature and role of those groups and societies in which decision making power is highly concentrated and centralised. Elitist theorists usually start from the basic premise that in every human institution there is an ordered system of a power with one group directly or indirectly exercising the major share of authority and control. In advanced and powerful societies—two classes of people appear—a class that rules and a class that

is ruled.[19] The first class always the less numerous, performs all political functions, monopolises power and enjoys the advantages that power brings, whereas, the second the more numerous class, is directed and controlled by the first. Every society has elite competing with each other job power which ultimately paves their way to formulate and execute public policies. (Mosca 1939). Fines has illustrated the elite position in a political system by the simile of an orange :

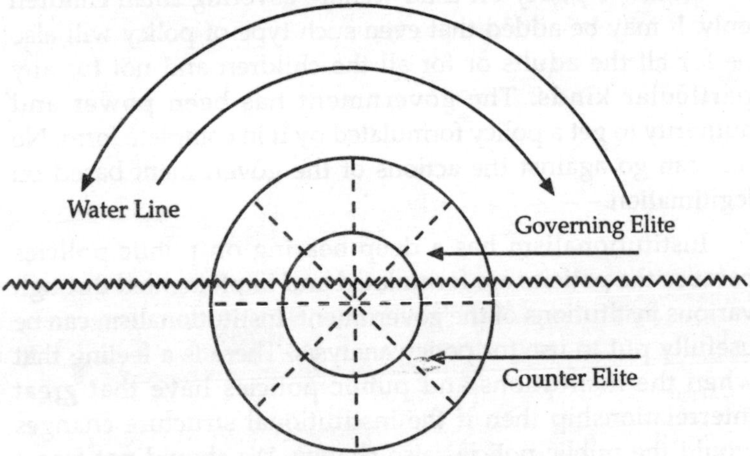

As per Finer, this orange with its skin representing the elite of society, floats in water, that portion of the skin that is above the waterline represents the governing elite, and the segments which it cover represents those associations in society which have succeeded in competition to have their leadership participate or hold office in the government. All those segments under the water-line, however, represent those associations which have lost their competition, and whose policies are temporarily being subordinated to those of the victorious ones, and the portions of peel that cover them represent, for society as a whole, the counter-elite that seeks to displace the governing elite at any point of time (Finer, 1962).

Elite theory has been summarized as such (Dye and Zeigler, 1970) :

1. Society is divided into the few who have power and the many who do not. Only a small number of persons allocate values for society, the masses do not decide policy.
2. The few who govern are not typical of the masses who are governed. Elites are drawn disproportionately from the upper socio-economic strata of society.
3. The movement of non-elites to elite positions must be slow and continuous to maintain stability and avoid revolution. Only non-elites who have accepted the basic elite consensus can be admitted to governing circles.
4. Elites share a consensus on the basic values of the social system and the preservation of the system.
5. Public policy does not reflect demands of the masses but rather the prevailing values of the elite. Changes in public policy will be incremented rather than revolutionary. Incremental changes permit responses to events that threaten a social system with a minimum of alteration or dislocation of the system.
6. Active elites are subject to relatively little direct influence from apathetic masses. Elites influence masses more than masses influence elites.

It becomes clear from the elite theory that it is a competition between the Elites in power and the counter-elites, attempting to come to power and the common masses, whose demands the public policies are formulated, are no where in determining the public policies. The policies are formulated by a ruling elite and the governmental officials and agencies carry those into effect.[20]

Implications

The implications of elite model are the following :

1. Policy is the product of elites and reflects their values and serving their ends. What is found in actual practice is that the demands of the people are not reflected that quantitatively as well as qualitatively for the

determination of public policy, as much as the concern and shade of elites. The redefinition and change in the public policies is not based on the demands of the masses but again the top echelon in the systems wants that for the protection of its own interests and value in the reshaped and modified policies.[21] Policies are more often amended but rarely changed. The change in the policies takes place only when the elites feel that the system as such is under threat. In order to save the system and to keep their position well intact in it, the elites change the policies. Again it is evident here that the change in the policy was because of the interests of the elites only and not that of the masses.

2. The protagonists of democracy as a rule of government often feel happy with the famous quotation "Democracy is government of the people, for the people and by the people." What we actually view is that in the government process, nowhere the common masses are taken into consideration. In the poor countries, the poverty is increasing day by day but the rich are accumulating wealth with great speed. Policy framers formulate policies on the demands of the people and these demands were laid down before the masses by the political parties of the time of electrons in the form of election manifestos. Masses had supported the party/ parties and their policies and have provided them with a line of action to work and formulate policies on those issues which were clarified or raised in the election manifestos. The question can be raised here how many political parties present dixerent programmes, especially in a system where multi-party system exists? It has been lightly said that the democratic institutions, elections, parties are important for their symbolic values only and nothing beyond that. It is always the elite which decides the issues for formulating policies on. Now, especially the democratic rule should be known as—Democracy is a government off the people, far the

people, and buy the people.[22] The participation of the people in rule of government is comparatively much more ensured and sought for in democracy rather than in Dictatorship and Military rule. Elite theory leads us to the point of concern that the less numerous in a political system rule over the majority in society and on the role of leadership on the issues of policy making that few govern the many.

10. *Functional Model* : Policy as a functional activity. Functionalism is an approach to political analysis characterised by its focus on functions performed by or within political systems. Functionalism is an umbrella term covering a variety of analytic modes. It sometimes means no more than the investigation of activities engaged in by some individual, groups or organization within a political system or the purpose served by such activities. This approach has been called electric functionalism.

For the purpose of policy analysis, the following categories of functional analysis will act as the base (Lasswell, 1956) :

1. *Intelligence* : How is the information on policy matters that comes to the attention of policy makers gathered and processed ?

2. *Recommendation* : How are recommendations alternatives for dealing with a given issue made and promoted ?

3. *Prescription* : How are general rules adopted or enacted, and by whom ?

4. *Invocation* : Who determines whether given behaviour contravenes rules or law and demand application of rules or laws thereto ?

5. *Application* : How are laws or rules actually applied or enforced ?

6. *Appraisal* : How is the operation of policies, their success or failure, appraised ? and

7. *Termination* : How are the original rules or laws terminated or continued in modified or changed form ?

We know public policy process as a pattern or course of activity. Right from the very start in the policy formulation process *i.e.*, how the information on policy matters that comes to the attention of policy makers gathered and processed upto the end *i.e.*, how the original rules or laws terminated, all the activities find place in the categories of functional analysis given by Lesswell. On the basis of these categories not only the specific or individual policies can be analysed but also a comparative analysis of all the policies in a given political system can be easily made. One can probe into how the various functions are performed, who performs them and what are their outcome and effects.[23]

11. *Group Model* : Group is a collectivity of individuals distinguished by some common attribute or shared relationship. Groups are categorized in many different ways. A formal or organised group, such as political party or an interest group, has recognised goals and structures affecting group interaction. An informal group lacks such explicit goals and organisational structure. A primary group is relatively small, collectivity that engages in frequent and direct interactions, whereas the members of secondary group interact infrequently and communicate mainly by indirect and impersonal means. A political interest group is a collection of those that seek to influence governmental policy in favour of some goal as associational, non-associational, institutional and anomic.

Group theory is an approach that seeks to explain political behaviour primarily through the study of the nature and interaction of social groups. In political system, group is regarded as the primary basis for all political activity and hence, for political analysis. As per the group theory, public policy is the product of the group struggle. Public policy in a political system is formulated on the basis of the equilibrium reached at the struggle of various groups prominently engaged in the process. From the groups theory point of view, public policy has been termed as—what may be called public policy is actually the equilibrium reached in the group struggle at any given moment and if represents a balance which the contending factions or groups constantly strive to tip in their favour.[24]

The effectiveness of the group or groups plays on important role in the enactment of various policies. On the basis of their strength in the legislature, the major policy formulation institution of the government, the groups are in a position to carry out their policies as accepted one. The policies which are made through in the legislature are faithfully carried out for implementation by the administrative agencies and the judiciary, and in the enactment of the policies it is primarity the group struggle, and the victory of the groups having more strength, which is importantly displayed in the attainment of its goals. For example, let us suppose that there are three groups known as A, B and C in the legislature having total membership of 100. Their strength is 40, 32 and 28 respectively. Group A having majority strength in the House proposes issue 'X' for formulating a policy on it. In case, group B and C remain disunited with each other and do not reach a point of agreement, then group A will have an edge over them and will get the issue through. But if group B and C after bargaining with each other reach a compromise then group A would be incapacitated to get a policy made on issue 'X'. Sometimes the group struggle and reaching certain agreements after adopting the policy of give and take does emerge even within one party or group composed of different sub-groups, factions or interest groups. Group theory aims at viewing all significant political activity with regard to group struggle policy formulators are termed as succumbing to pressures of groups, such as bargaining, negotiating and compromising. Another important dimension of the group struggle is the maintenance of equilibrium in the system. The competition among the groups does not permit any group to become absolutely powerful in a system. Hence, they keep on checking the activities of each other. The ultimate gainers in such like situations are the individuals who are benefited by having sound policies in the game of group struggle and equilibrium.

Policy as Efficient Goal Attainment : Gold is the condition or end that an individual or group desires to achieve. Political goals may relate to the allocation of rewards within a system, to bringing about a certain event or avoiding it, to changing an intangible element. The nature of a political system, environmental factors, the personalities of decision-makers, ideological considerations, and capability, etc. analyses to help to determine the number and kinds of goals sought by political actors.[25]

A reasonable and logical policy aims at the attainment of 'net value achievement' to the maximum extent (Havemen, 1970). 'Net value achievement' can be attained when the policy makers have complete knowledge about the values required to be cared for in the policies.[26] Value as a concept what is desirable or good, or in some usages, the good or desired thing itself. Values reflect what a person wants—a goal, preference, a desired end state. Values are internal, subjective concepts that postulate standards of morality, ethics and personal preference. In the light of the traditions, customs, environmental factors, demands as per the requirements of the time factor and other related things, the values of the society emerge. A policy termed sound, safe, logical, reasonable, rational, and efficient when the percentage of the value attained by it proportionately positive than the percentage of the values the policy has sacrificed. For bringing out an efficient and sound policy, the following factors must be kept in active considerations by the policy formulators. To be aware of the Society's value preferences, to be in the know of all the policy alternatives available. By keeping in view all the consequences of each policy alternative, By calculating the ratio of achieved to sacrificed societal values for each policy alternative, and by selecting the most efficient policy alternative (Dror, 1968).

12. *System Bodel* : Policy as system output. Systems theory or model treats politics as a set of interactions occurring within, but analytically distinct from the larger social environment. Systems analysis provides a number of conceptual categories

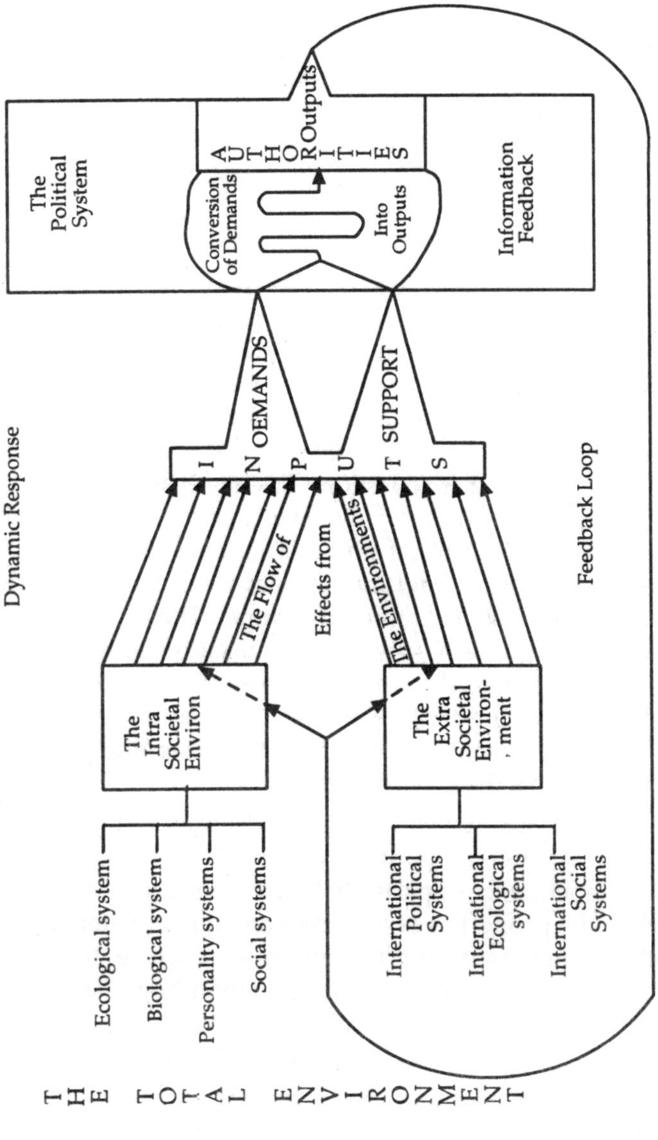

"Model of Political System", Easton, David, A Framework for Political Analysis. (Newjersy, Prentice-Hall, 1965)

for describing and analysing political behaviour. Some of the more salient concepts are system, sub-system, environment, boundary, input, output, conversion process and feed back.

1. *The Political System* : The term "political system" has become increasingly common in the titles and monographs in the field of comparative politics. The older texts used such terms as "government", "nation", or "state" to describe what we call a political system. This new terminology reflects a new way of looking at political phenomena. It includes some new names for old things. The older terms—state, government, nation—are limited by legal and institutional meanings.

The concept of "political system" has acquired wide currency because it directs attention to the entire scope of political activities within a society, regardless of where in the society such activities may be located. What is the political system? How do we define its boundaries? What gives the political system its special identity? Many political scientists have dealt with these questions. Easton speaks of "authoritative allocation of values",[27] Lasswell and Kaplan of "severe deprivations", Dahl, of power, rule and authority. All these definitions imply legitimate, heavy sanctions, the lightful power to punish, to enforce, to compel. Thus, public recreation facilities are usually supported by taxation, and any violation of the regulations governing their use is a legal offense. We are not, then, saying that the political system is concerned solely with force, violence, or compulsion, rather that its relation to coercion is its distinctive quality.

2. *The Sub-System* : The second important concept of the political system is sub-system. A system implies the interdependence of parts. By "interdependence" we mean that when the properties of one component in a system change, all other components and the system as a whole are affected. A change in one part leads to corresponding change in other parts, other sub-sets, sub-collections[28] etc.

3. *Boundary* : A third aspect of the concept of "system" is the notion of boundary. A system starts somewhere and stops somewhere[29]. In dealing with social systems, of which political systems, the problem of boundary is not that easy. Social

system are made up not of individuals, but of roles. A family, for example, consists of the roles of mother and father, husband and wife, sibling and sibling. The family is only one set of interacting roles for its members, who also may have roles outside the family in schools, business firms and churches. In the same sense a political system is made up of the interacting roles of nations, subjects, voters, as the case may be, with legislators, bureaucrats and judges. The same individuals who perform roles in the political system perform roles in other social systems such as the economy, the religious community, the family and voluntary associations. As individuals expose themselves to political communication, form interest groups, vote or pay taxes, they shift from non-political to political roles. One might say that on election day as citizens leave their farms, plants, and offices to go to the polling places, they are crossing the boundary from the economy to the polity.[30]

Another example of a shift in the boundary of the political system might occur when inflation reduces the real income of certain groups in the population. When such a change in the economic situation of particular groups gets converted into demands for public policy or for changes in political personnel, there is an interaction between the economy and the polity. Somewhere in this process, a boundary is crossed from one system to another from the economic system to the political system.

The boundaries of the political systems are subject to relatively large fluctuations. During wartime the boundaries become greatly extended as large numbers of men are recuited into military service, as business firms are subjected to regulations, and as internal security measures are taken. In an election the boundaries again are greatly extended as voters become politicians for a day. With the return to more normal conditions, the boundaries of the political system contract.

4. *Input, Conversion, Output* : This is the fourth and the last concept of the political system. The problem of boundaries taken on special significance because systems theory usually divides interaction process into three phases—input conversion, output. Any set of interacting parts—any system—

which is affected by factors in its environment may be viewed in this fashion. The inputs and outputs, which involve the political system with other social systems, are transactions between the system and its environment, the conversion processes are internal to the political system. When we talk about the sources of inputs, their number, content, and intensity, and how they enter the political system and of the number and content of outputs and how they leave the political system and affect other Social Systems, we shall in effect be talking about the boundaries of the political system. The units which make up all social systems, including political systems, are roles.

System implies patterned interactions or persisting relationships among political entities. A system that constitutes an element of a larger system is called a sub-system. The setting within which a system occurs in its environment. The analytical line that separates the system from its environment is the boundary of the system. A system receives inputs from its environment in the form of demands upon the system and supports for its functioning. Through the operations of systems the inputs are subjected to conversion process, which leads to systems outputs embodying rules to be enforced or policies to be implemented. When system outputs affect the environment so as to modify inputs, feedback occurs.

Public policies may be regarded as an output of political system in response to the demands coming out of the environment of that system. Political system has been defined as the one which allocates values by means of its policies that are binding on the society by virtue of being authoritative.[31] Policy is clearly authoritative when the feeling prevails that it must or ought to be obeyed and the policies, whether formal or effective, are accepted as binding (Easton 1957). As per systems theory, the outputs (*i.e.*, public policies) of a system are those which emerge through a definite procedure. By keeping in view the feed back model of political system given by David Easton, one can understand that the demands are put into a process of conversion for bringing out the outputs. Systems theory depicts public policy as an output of the system. The policy formulators or the governmental agencies engaged in the policy making process have to keep in mind the values, preferences and desires of the people. Of course, whatever policy, whether serving the net value achievement upto the maximum or not, would be a binding on all and everybody shall have to accept it because of its being authoritative, but if the system would always be bringing or making such kind of policies then probably such an arrangement on the part of the policy makers will not last long. Moreover, when we analyse the system approach and view it from the angle of policy formulating and implementing process, we become aware of the factor that only those demands would be put through for making policies which are having the genuinity in them and which are easily supported.

Demands and supports constitute inputs in a policy making process in a political system.[32] In order to protect and satisfy their interests, demands and claims are made on the political system for taking action by the individuals and groups. Support is given when the actions and decisions made by the authoritative political system are lawfully and obediently accepted by the individuals and the groups. Public policy is constituted of such on authoritative allocation of values. Certain issues in whole or some parts of certain issues which could not be translated as Public Policy (*i.e.* output) are again put through the same process which is known as feed back process. More demands emerge out of policy outputs which amounts to further policy input and so on and this public policy process goes on in an endless manner.[33]

The utility of systems theory in terms of public policy formulation cannot be minimised because it makes us to know the process as such. Simultaneously, it cautions us to probe into certain relevant points to know the manner in which environmental inputs affect the content of public policy and the nature of Political system. Public policy, affects the environment and subsequent demands for action, forces or factors in the environment act to generate demands upon the political system, political system is able to convert demands into public policy and preserve itself over time (Anderson, 1979).

Utility of Models

In the preceding pages an attempt has been made to analyse public policy process on the basis of different models of policy analysis, such as policy as institutional activity, policy as elite preference, policy as functional activity, policy as group equilibrium, policy as efficient goal attainment, and policy as system output. It is rather difficult to say which of these models is better than others. Every model emphasises different and distinct aspects of politics and policy making process and appears to be highly beneficial and significant for some purposes. The practitioners and theorists of politics and political science respectively have preferred for one model or the other, of course suiting their point of view, yet it is not easy for one, who is interested in analysing policy making process, to prefer rigidly one model or other. General criterion for evaluating the utility of these models is as such (Dye, 1975).

1. Certainly the utility of a model lies in its ability to order and simplify political life so that one can think about it more clearly and understand the relationships in the real world. Yet, too much simplification can lead to inaccuracies in thinking about reality. If a concept is too narrow or identifies only superficial phenomena, it is not able to be used for explaining public policy. On the other hand, if a concept is too broad and suggests overly complex relationships, it may become so complicated and unmanageable that it is not really an aid to understanding. In other words, some theories of politics for the analysis of public policy may be too complex to be helpful, while others may be too simplistic.[34]

2. A model should identify the really significant aspects of public policy. It should direct attention away from irrelevant variables or circumstances, and focus upon the real causes and significant causes of public policy. Of course, what is real, relevant, and significant is to some extent a function of

individuals personal values. The utility of a model is related to its ability to identify what it is that is really important aspect of public policy.

3. A model should normally be nearer reality, that is, it ought to have real empirical referents. Difficulty is expected of a process that does not really occur, or symbolises phenomena that do not exist in real world. The unrealistic concepts, if they succeed in directing attention to why they are unrealistic, should not be quickly dismissed. For example, no one contends that government decision making is completely rational, public officials do not always act to maximise societal values and minimise societal costs. Yet the concept of rational decision making may be still useful, if it makes us realise how irrational government decision making really is and prompts to inquire about why it is rational.[35]

4. A model should also communicate something meaningful. If too many disagree over the meaning of a concept, its utility in communication is diminished. For example, if one really agreed on what constitutes on Elite, then the concept of elite does not mean the something to every one. If one defines on 'elite' as democratically elected public officials who are representative of the general public, then he is communicating a different idea in using the term than one who defines on elite as an unrepresentative minority that makes decisions for society based on its own interests.

5. A model should help to direct inquiry into, research into public policy. A model should be operational, that is, it should refer directly to real world phenomena that can be observed, measured, and verified.

6. A model approach should suggest an explanation of public policy. It should suggest hypothesis about the causes and consequences of public policy—hypotheses that can be tested against real-world data. A model that merely describes public policy is not as useful as a model that explains public policy, or at least suggests some possible explanation.[36]

REFERENCES

1. Lipset, S.M., Politics and Social Sciences, New York, Wiley, 1966.
2. We cannot escape from politics. It is unavoidable and inevitable. It affect us directly or indirectly everyday.
3. Ranney Austin (ed.), Political Science and Public Policy, Chicago, Markhan, 1968.
4. Public policy means choosing of one alternative from the many alternatives.
6. Easton David, A System Analysis of Political Life, New York, Wilsey, 1965.
7. Sufficient information is essential for the formulation of correct and authentic public policy.
8. Rein Martin, Social Science and Public Policy, Pennsylvania, Offset Paperback Mfrs., 1976.
9. Tawney, R.H., Equality, New York Allen and Unwin, 1952.
10. Public policy can be interpreted in many ways. Its goals are open.
11. Landau, M., "On the Basis of Metaphor in Political Analysis" in Social Research, Vol. 28, 1961.
12. Coalition Governments are nothing but the marriages of convenience.
13. Wildavsky, Aaron, Speaking Truth to Power, New York, Wiley 1979.
14. Dye, Thomas R., Understanding Public Policy, Englewood Cliffs, Prentice Hall, 1975.
15. In the incremental policies, means are more important than the ends.
16. Somit Albert and Tamenhaus, Joseph, The Development of American Political Science, From Burgees to Behaviouralism, Boston, 1967.
17. Mosca, G., The Ruling Class, New York, Mcgraw Hill, 1939.
18. Finer, H., Theory and Practice of Modern Government, New York, Methuen 1962.
19. Legitimacy is one of the crucial element of the political system. Legitimacy is closely related to effectiveness.
20. Dye, Thomas, R. and Zeigler, Harmon, The Irony of Democracy, Belmount, California, Wadsworth, 1970.

21. Lasswell, Harold D., The Decision Process, Madison, University of Maryland, 1956.
22. Truman, David B., The Governmental Process, New York, Knopf, 1951.
23. Lethem, Earl, The Group Basis of Politics, in Eulau, Heing, *et al.* (eds.) Political Behaviour, New York, Free Press, 1956.
24. Dror, Yehezkel, Public Policy Making Re-examined, Part IV, "An Optional Model of Public Policy Making", San Fransico, Chandler, 1968.
25. Wtto, Wtto Chronicle, November 1977, pp. 441-448.
26. UN, 'Administration of National Development Planning : Report of Meeting Experts, ST/TAD/M/27.
27. Quoted in Waldo, Ideas and Issues in Public Administration, p. 71.
28. Appleby Paul H., Policy and Administration, p. 71.
29. Robson, W.A., 'India Revisited' in Political Quarterly, Oct.-Dec. 1960, p. 436.
30. The boundaries of all the systems are not fixed and constant. There is an interaction between them.
31. Authoritative means it must be obeyed by the people. Decisions are made by the few elites in the society and they are binding on all the members of the society. People must abide by the decisions.
32. Demands and supports are the two important forces of the political system.
33. Public policy is endless and it is performed continuously and regularly.
34. Some models of public policy are too broad and complex and others are too simple.
35. Rational policy making is an important task of the government of the day.
36. Model's are useful in explaining and predicting of some problems and suggests the possible solutions.

3

PUBLIC POLICY AND ENVIRONMENT

Public policies—whether substantive, regulatory, distributive, or ethical, occur in a given system, whether it is democratic in nature or dictatorial in kind. Various procedures and means are adopted in a given system to formulate polices on certain issues. According to the capabilities and authority of the system, the issues translated into policies are implemented and enforced in an effective manner. According to systems theory policy formulation process cannot be appropriately understood without considering the environment in which it takes place.

Environment is the setting or surrounding conditions within which any object or system occurs. The environment of a political system includes human and non-human factors, both tangible and intangible. For example, geographical factors, other social systems, ideologies, customs and institutions may all be features of the environment of a political system. In systems analysis, the environment consists of all phenomena that affect the functioning of system and that are not part of the system.[1] The governmental agencies and actors cannot ignore the environmental factors and forces at the time of making policies. Rather the policies are framed according to the environment and its factors around. Since the origin of the state and emergence of the government as an institute to manage the affairs of the state, we find that the decisions and actions have been taken keeping in view the environment in which they the government exist. The culture, traditions, customs, social factors, economic considerations, ethnic issues and factors all have to be focused upon at the time of making policy decisions by the government. The concept of nation-state is now changing into that of internation state, because of the states being highly dependent on each other.[2] Pondering over this consideration even the other nations become a part of the environment of a given political system, because the trade, foreign and defence policies are being made on these issues.

Whether we consider Almond's model or Easton's model, we find the demands and support factors in view. When we probe deep into all or any one of these models, we become aware of the fact that ultimately the things start and end with the environment.[3] We have the tendency to go upto the maximum and one reaches there only in terms of policy making when one tries to view the aspects from the environmental conditions and situations. In this chapter, the focus of discussion would be on certain environmental factors and the role of institutions.

1. *Political Culture* : Culture is an aggregate of learned, socially transmitted behaviour patterns characteristic of a society.[4] The culture of a social group is developed and maintained through formal and informal learning knowledge, language, beliefs, customs, traditions, institutions, in sum the totality of social experience. A political system is shaped by related cultural factors and may, in turn, promote cultural change by influencing other behaviour patterns of society.[5] Political culture is the pattern of orientations towards government and politics within a political system. It generally cannotes the psychological dimensions of political behaviour, beliefs, feelings, and evaluative orientations. A political is the product of historical experience of the whole society as well as the personal experience that contribute to socialization of each individual. Culture is the pattern of individual attitude and orientation towards politics among the members of a political system (Almond, 1966).[6] In a given society, the individuals have an almost identical emotional values, ethical and moral principles and intellectual capacities. All these

aspects pave the way to the formation of a general culture of the society. Certain aspects of the general culture of a society are especially concerned with how government ought to be conducted and what shall it try to do. This sector of the culture we call political culture (Beer, 1962). The political culture is not static but it is dynamic.[7] It is a continuous process depending upon the needs arising from within the political system and also being imposed and imparted from outside. Through the process of political socialization, political culture gets transmitted from one generation to another.[8] The major agents involved in this transmission of culture from one generation to another are family, school, peer-groups, religious institutions, youth organisations, employing agencies, channels of mass communication etc. A political culture is composed of the attitudes, beliefs, emotions and values of society that relates to the political system and to political issues (Ball, 1971). The individuals behave to the tune of political culture and their belief, attitudes, and values are reflected in their behaviour and approach towards politics, policies and policy administration.

A division of political culture differentiating between parochial, subject, and participant, political culture has been made (Almond, 1965).

1. *The Parochial Political Culture* : It could be found in highly traditional society based upon such a simple thinking and not showing any inclination towards the political system, the process of input, based on political socialization, interest aggregation, interest articulation, political communication, and output process, having included in it rule making, rule interpreting and rule enforcing, and the amount of specialisation required in dealing with various functions. In other words, nothing is expected by the parochial political culture from the political system.[9] Parochials are those people who manifest little or no awareness of the national political systems. Such individuals are to be found in any society, but in modern Western societies they are relatively rare. Parochials may be found in certain areas, not yet affected by the national polity.

2. *Subjects Political Culture* : In the subject political culture the people have quantitative orientations to the political system in general and to its output activities in particular. It normally exists in countries which are being ruled over by others. Such dependent countries either accept the policy formulated by their 'Governors' to the fullest extent by taking it legitimate and showing their loyalty to the system, or they refute and reject the policies considering those as being forcefully imposed upon them.[10] Such culture is found where the individuals have general awareness of the governmental authority and they either approve of it or disapprove it. Subjects are those individuals who are oriented to the political system and the impact which its outputs, such as welfare benefits, laws, etc., may have upon their lives, but who are not oriented to participation in the input structures.

3. *Participant Political Culture* : The participant political culture, as is implied by the term, means where the individuals have a high ranking understanding of the political system, its functional areas, like input-output process, role and effectiveness of public opinion and well meant participation of the individuals in the process of the government. It normally exists in highly developed societies. Evaluation and criticism of the system exist at all levels.[11] Participants are those individuals who are oriented to the input structures and processes, and engage in, or view themselves as potentially engaging in the articulation of demands and the making of decisions.[12]

Political culture as a part of the environment of the political system definitely has a bearing on the process of policy making as such. The norms, values, attitudes, beliefs, traditions and customs, which remain in practical applicability for quite a long time turn into political culture. We have noted this also that the political culture is transmitted from one generation to another through the process of political socialization. Our point of interest here is to know how political culture affects policy making process. Of course, where the political culture would be parochial, there it would have no impressions on the minds of policy formulators regarding the policies to be framed by keeping certain well established factors in view. Like this, we cannot find considerable effect of subject political culture on policy-making because in such like situations also, the subjects have the culture to either accept or reject the outputs, or policies made by the government. But in this situation, the political masters cannot always go on making the policies which would be rejected or refused by the masses to be implemented upon. In participant political culture, where the citizens are highly aware policy-makers have to give great attention to the cultural norms and factors. Let us analyse it from another angle. We have found where the political culture is narrower and parochial, there the policy formulators have got a free hand, where the culture is such by which the output processes are understood, there the policy formulators have fifty per cent victory to their credit in comparison to hundred per cent in parochial political culture societies and where the participative political culture exists there the policy makers have very little at their disposal.

2. *Social and Economic Factors* : Much of the literature in politics implies that the division of party-vote, the level of interparty competition, the level of voter participation, and the degree of malapportionment in legislative bodies all influence public policy. Economic development shapes both political systems and policy outcomes, and most of the association that occurs between system characteristics and policy outcomes can be attributed to the influence of economic development. Differences in policy choices of states with different types of political systems turn out to be largely a product of differing socio-economic levels rather than a direct product of political variables level of urbanization, industrialization, income and education appear to be more influencial in shaping policy outcomes than political system characteristics (Dye, 1966).

Political system has been termed as a set of a interactions abstracted from the totality of social behaviour. The idea of social matrix implies that political interactions have their origin in, and are shaped by the social setting. Political roles are thus to be examined in relationship to other social roles and to the group and class structure of society.[13] No government or political masters can steal show for longer period successfully by ignoring the social values and beliefs prevailing in the society. The social factors have an important place in the overall environmental factors which the policy makers have to actively consider at the time of policy formulation.[13] The old traditions, customs, and religious norms all are parts of the social factors which the policy makers are found to take into consideration. Of course, it is a fact that because of the authoritative allocation of values, the public policies made can be implemented but in democratic nations such an attitude of the political masters does not pay them in the long run. An example to this effect can be quoted that of 'Operation Bluestar' ordered by the Government in June 1984, whereby the Golden Temple, Amritsar and various other shrines of the Sikhs were attacked by the armed forces. The price the Congress Party had to pay for this action was the thumping victory of the Akali Dal (Longowal) in the state Assembly elections held in September 1985. No section of the society will ever tolerate any such kind of policy to be formulated which hurts their traditions, customs or religion.

Public policies can be usefully viewed as arising out of conflicts between different groups of people, private and official, possessing different interests and desires. Economic activity is the prime source of conflict in the political system.[14] If we say that economic activities are the most dominating ones in the overall ecology of a political system, it would not be a tall claim. Nations are known and ranked in the international sphere on the basis of their economic strength.[15] Within the boundaries of a system, *i.e.*, within the administrative, territorial jurisdiction of a country, and outside that, is, its relationship with other countries, the government has to formulate policies governing the economic conditions within and outside the country. It is certain that every citizen will definitely need and aspire for such like policies whereby he is provided with the provisions to meet the basic economic needs like food, clothing and shelter.[16] It is for all purposes the duty of the government to make such types of policies through which it could get the people their basic economic necessities. Man is known as a social animal by nature and necessity.[17] One of the major reasons for the man to join the institution of state and to respect, obey and care for that was for the fulfilment of his prime needs and necessities. Hence, it becomes the overall concern of the policy makers to make the policies which could help people in solving their economic problems and difficulties.

But the focus of discussion here is not what the government should do in respect to the economic activities, but how the governments are affected by the economic causes and factors for determining policies. We have noted down the point of Dye that the political variables are subordinate to socio-economic variables. It is not the political ideologies or claims which will provide food to the citizens but in turn it would be economic resources which will provide the same.[18] The role of big business houses in getting the policies formulated to their own interests is quite commonly known and of course, it is always the weaker group in the game which will seek for government intervention in the shape of one policy or the other. It does not mean that the policies made by the government are always suiting the interests of the big business houses. Because, if this is to be the situation then in the times to come the party in government cannot come to power.

Propositions : There are certain propositions which emerge out of our analysis pertaining to policy making and economic activity :

1. It is agreed that the political variables are subordinate to economic variable. The economic factors and activities have to be kept in view while formulating the policies.
2. The big business houses can provide financial help to the party at the time of elections, but what about the votes. If we have accepted the primacy of economic

variables over political variables, it does not amount that the political variables are absolutely or completely insignificant and unimportant. All political, social and economic considerations go hand in hand in running the showing the show effectively.

3. In democracies, the people elect the government, for what ? Is it not to provide them those goods and services which they cannot manage for themselves ? Of course, it does not mean that the government is having any magic stick with the help of which those policies would be enacted which will enrich the masses of material resources upto the maximum. But certainly government can make such policies whereby taking the physical and social assistance of the masses the level of economic development can be increased. For all these scores to be settled, is it possible to say that the policy-making is not affected by the social and economic factors, or to say that the social and economic factors have no role to play *vis-a-vis* policy-making.

Governmental Policy-Making Agencies : Policies are made by the governmental institutions. These institutions have legal authority to their credit, this authority of the governments become the forceful factors in the operation of the policy implementation. Of course, such like institutions are under the overall control of the political parties and the pressure groups actively placed in the system. The government institutions engaged in the process of policy making are legislatures, executives, administrative agencies, and courts. Certainly these institutions are very much parts and pascels of the given environment of the system.[19] The role and functions being performed by all these institutions are different from each other. Of course a distinction can be made between the elementary policy making agencies and secondary policy making agencies. Elementary agencies are those which have direct authorization to frame the policies and the secondary agencies are those which get the powers to act by seeking authority from the elementary agencies. For example the parliament does not seek authority from any other agency to act, whereas the administrative agencies have to depend on elementary agencies like, parliament for acting in a particular manner.

1. *Legislatures* : The legislature occupies a prominent and pivotal position in the policy making process and is rather superior to the other governmental institutions involved in the sphere. The primary and the most important function of the state is policy making and this is undertaken by the legislature. The executive will take action only when the policy formulated by the legislature will come into being and the judiciary will also make judgments on the basis of the laws and policies enacted by the legislature. Every executive and judicial act involves primarily an enactment by the legislature. The legislature formulates and express the will of the state through the policies.[20] Being representative in nature, the legislature enacts the general rules in the forms of policies. The policies of the state prescribed the manner in which the people are expected to live in a politically organised society. However, it cannot be taken for granted that the legislatures have all the powers pertaining to policy making. It is said that the legislatures have been reduced to mere sound boards or mere rubber-stamp endorsing policies already framed by the executive (Jain, 1975). Whatever the case may be in different political systems, still the legislatures formalise the policies.

The functions of the legislature vary or differ from each other in different political set-ups. In U.S.A. the legislature has immense powers because of the fact that the executive in the president cannot considerably influence upon the Congress because of the theory of separation of powers. Of course, through his party men indirect influence can be exercised by him. Moreover, the American Congress has a strong committee mechanism. The Congressional Committees are known as 'little legislatures'.

In a parliamentary form of political systems, the position of the legislature seems to be apparently superior to that of the executive, because the executive in the cabinet is responsible to the parliament, as in the case of England and India, for all its acts and can stay on as long as it enjoys the confidence of the parliament.[21] But the actual position is somewhat different. The executive has the support of the majority of the members in the parliament and so the executive can get policies formulated on any issue by the parliament. It does not amount to the conclusion that the parliaments do not do any fruitful task in policy-formulation in England and India. The important functions performed by them include deliberating, scrutinizing, criticising and publicizing the policies of the government and the implications of those policies for the government.

The Supreme Soviet the legislature in the U.S.S.R. does not possess much powers to legislate upon the issues, neither it has time for that legislate upon the issues, neither it has time for that because it meets for only a span of few days twice a year. Therefore, it has no other option than to ratify or confirm the decisions made by the party officials. The National People's Congress also in peoples Republic of China does not enjoy the usual importance and prestige enjoyed by its counterparts in U.S.A., England and India. It has formal and secondary role to play. The policies are determined by the Chinese Communist Party and are submitted before the legislature for obtaining formal approval only.[22]

The analysis of the position of legislatures in different political systems made above reveals that the role, importance, and significance of the legislative bodies vary from highly maximum to utmost minimal. But it is true that whether it is people's Republic of China or U.S.S.R., where the legislatures are only the formal bodies, still the policies though determined by the party officials are ratified by the legislature. To its contrary, we have known the actual powers, pertaining to the policy-making, vested with the Congress in U.S.A., parliament in Britain and India.

2. *The Executive* : In the present times the real political power rests with the executive organ of the government and the administration serving it. It would not be wrong to say that we are residing in an executive-centered era. The executive

leadership mean a lot both in the making of the policy and its proper execution. If we view the executive in broader sense, the executive includes not only the head of the state but also at the Ministers and the whole subordinate executive and administrative functionaries who perform various tasks in the system. Of course, our present discussion shall relate the narrower sense of the term which includes the political executives which have a significant role to play in the policy making.

In a parliamentary form of democracy, real executive powers lie with the Prime-Minister and his cabinet and not with the king or queen, as in Britain or with the President, as in India. The king or queen in Britain, and the president in India are only the nominal heads of the states.[23] Of course, to legislate on the issues for the purpose of enacting policies is the job of the legislatures to whom even the real executive are also responsible. But in actual practice the things are altogether different and we find that the issues on which the policies are made are thought over by the executive and submitted to the legislatures for approval. More rightly so, the executive is embodied with all the powers and it is rather obligatory on its part to get policies formulated on the points whereby it could satisfy the people in a given system by making policies on the issues which serve the needs and aspirations of the people. If we analyse the actual working of the political systems, we can easily understand that the policy issues are determined by the executives. In India, various political parties contest the elections and on the basis of their strength in the parliament, especially in Lok Sabha, the party having majority comes to power. The issues are submitted before the legislature for making policies on those. It is done both by the party in power and by the opposition parties. Of course, the issues covering important aspects are raised by the government *i.e.*, the political executive and not by the opposition groups in the House. And even if the opposition group will do so, it would no be carried out because the executive is having majority in the legislature. It clearly reveals that it is the executive which determines the major policy issues for policy-making.

Though the right of proposing legislation is shared by the Diet with the Cabinet in Japan, yet the cabinet initiates most of the legislative measures.

In this manner the Japanese Cabinet like the executives in U.S.A., Britain, India and France is better equipped than legislative bodies to handle legislation of a complex nature. Policy making today has the requirement of technical and legal competence and this is more likely to be found in the executive organ of the government than anywhere else.[24]

The executive in the most of the underdeveloped and in some of the developing countries, exercise more influence in policy making in comparison to most of the developed countries. Because there are few policy issues, a larger proportion of them can reach the cabinet level in developing countries, because there is often no professional civil service (Dror, 1968). In countries like U.S.S.R. and People's Republic of China, the executive policy prevails. The leading and dominating role of the communist party in all fields of economic, social and cultural activity is the political basis of U.S.S.R.[25] No important political or organisational problem is ever decided by the Soviets and other mass orgnizations without directions from the party. Both the internal and external policy of the country is determined by the politbureau of the party. The Chinese system is also almost similar to that of U.S.S.R.

3. *Administrative Agencies* : As the legislatures and executives have different role in policy-making in various countries of the world and as they differ so far their actual powers and functions are concerned, similarly the administrative agencies also differ with each others in various political systems on the basis of features, *viz.*, size and complexity, hierarchical organisation, and level of autonomy. No problem is more momentous four the modern democratic state than its capacity to develop rational, responsible, goal-oriented policy. In various fields, including the foreign and defence policies—which are the most crucial ones—the staff work on which well conceived public policy must depend can

scarcely be supplied elsewhere than in the government departments. Accordingly, a major task of the administrative agencies is the formulation of policy proposals for consideration by the political executive and the legislature. The capacity of the administrative agencies to perform rationally and responsibly the task of formulating the policy alternative for politically responsible superiors is the major criterion of efficiency. The doctrine of the political supremacy of the elected over the non-elected branch of the government has inspired the delusion that to be politically supreme the legislature must not only make final decisions on policy but must also have primacy in the whole process of policy-making that the administrative agencies should be an instrument rather than a brain. Constitutionalism itself demands that the political will be limited by procedure. An important addition to the constitutional arsenal lies in the potentialities of administrative agencies. Power must be commensurative with responsibility.[25] Knowledge expands power, but in doing so, imposes limitations. For good or bad, we know the fund of knowledge in the administrative agencies will be a source of power.[26]

Though the common understanding is that the administrative agencies implement or enforce or execute or carryout the policies made by the political masters, yet with administration getting blended with politics, the role of administrative agencies has increased and now they are being significantly involved in policy-making. The concept of welfare state has decidedly increased the work load of the executive and legislature on making policies pertaining to numerous fields. More so, the legislators do not have proper and appropriate expertise for developing the policies.[27] Because of great amount of work, shortage of time, and lack of adequate expertise and knowledge, the legislature, frequently pass on rule making powers to administrative agencies. As a result of this, many decisions involving political and policy consequences are made by the administrative agencies. Proposals to legislate on various issues are also made by the administrative agencies in countries like U.S.A., Britain, and India.

4. *The Courts* : Legislation is the task of the legislatures but the courts and the judicial organs in a system also legislate. It is not a fiction but a fact that judges do legislate.[28]. Whenever the law is silent or unclear or it does not fall in consistency with some other policy of the political system, it is decided by the court what the policy is and what policy should prevail. To this effect the courts are guided by the values of equity and justice. The courts also play an effective role in stabilising and supporting the existing political system. The court decisions provide legitimacy to the governmental institutions outputs in various policies. Therefore, for the smooth running of the system, the attitude of the courts should not be of an obstructive or destructive nature.[29] If it is obligatory or compulsory on the part of the judiciary to legitimise the policies framed by the executive and legislature, then it becomes the duty of the political masters to see that the administration of justice is not endangered and the impartiality and independence of the courts is maintained.

In some of the political systems, the perform a noteable task in policy-making. By exercising the powers of judicial review, the courts have affected the nature and content of public policy. Judicial review is the power of the courts to declare acts of legislative and executive branches unconstitutional[30]. It is based on the assumption that the constitution is the supreme law, that acts contrary to the constitution are void, and that the judiciary is the guardian of the constitution. The unique power of the courts was originated in the U.S.A. Nowhere in the world the courts play a greater role in the policy-making as in U.S.A. The federal judiciary of the U.S.A. is the third member of the government trinity and is not less important than the other two. The power of judicial review was originated in U.S.A. The Supreme Court of the U.S.A. has played its significant role in shaping the policy. The Supreme Court of U.S.A. invalidated the National Security Act (1933). The court held unconstitutional the prayers in public schools, segregated school systems etc. The powers of the court to declare the policies made by the congress null and void has prevented the

Congress to make any such policy which will hamper the constitutional characteristics.

In Britain the laws passed and the policies made by the parliament are beyond the jurisdiction of any judicial review. No court in England can pass the verdict declaring the Act of Parliament as unconstitutional, null and void and ultra-vires.

As per Article 13 of the Constitution of India all laws, it includes ordinances, order, bye-law, rule, regulation, notification, custom or usage, in force in the territory of India immediately before the commencement of Indian constitution, in so far as they are inconsistent with the provisions of the part, dealing with the Fundamental rights of the citizens, shall to the extent of such inconsistency, be void. The state shall not make any laws which takes away or abridges the rights conferred in the Fundamental rights, and any law made in contravention of this clause shall, to the extent of contravention, be void. Therefore, the power of judicial review is clearly engrafted into the Indian Constitution.[31]

Of course, the courts in other countries as Japan, Australia, West Germany, and Canada have powers to review the policies framed by the legislatures, but these countries, judiciaries do not have as much powers as are there in U.S.A. and India, where the courts can exercise influence on policy-making. The courts also have in their jurisdictional areas to give interpretations and decisions on the policies and issues which have conflicting interpretations. The ones given by court are considered to be final unless again it is reviewed by the court only.

5. *Public Policy and Democracy* : The most conspicuous difference between authoritarianism and democratic regimes is that in democratic governments citizens choose or elect their top policy-makers in genuine elections. Some political scientists speculate that voting in genuine elections may be important method of citizens influence on policy not so much because it actually permits citizens to choose their officials and to some degree instruct these officials on policy, but because the

existence of genuine elections puts a stamp of approval on citizen participation. Indirectly, therefore, the fact of elections enforces on proximate policy makers a rule that citizens wishes count in policy making (Lindbloom, 1968).

Democracy is a system of government in which ultimate political authority is vested in the people.[32] The term is derived from the Greek word "demos" (The people) and "Kratos" (authority). Democracy may be direct, as practical in ancient Athens or indirect and representative. The democratic creed includes the following concepts. Individualism, which holds that the primary task of government is to enable each individual to achieve the highest potential of development, liberty, which allows each individual the greatest amount of freedom consistent with order, equality, which maintains that all men are equal and have equal rights and opportunities, and fraternity, which postulates that individuals will no misuse their freedom but will cooperate in creating a wholesome society.[33] As a political system, democracy starts with the assumption of popular sovereignty, vesting ultimate political power in the people. It presupposes that man can control his destiny, that he can make moral judgments and practical decisions in his daily life. Democracy requires a decision-making system based on majority rule, with minority rights protected. Effective guarantees of freedom of speech, press, religion, assembly, petition, and equality before the law are indispensable to a democratic form of government. Politics, parties and politicians are the catalystic agents that make democracy workable.[34]

Democracy is a form of government it is a kind of economy, it is an order of society, it is a way of life, it is all these things together. Initially the democracy was only a political concept but now its boundaries have had manifold expressions and induced in it are the social, economic, moral and ethical ideas and characteristic attributes are rational empiricism, emphasis on individual, law behind law, thrust upon means, discussion, and contest in human relations and human being equality. Democracy, having its frontiers expanded, lays emphasis on society as a whole rather than on state as an institution. It has included in it all the factors within affecting or making the environment within which the political system has to operate and make policies in the light of the demand and pressure of genuine nature arising out of the individual needs and requirements. Democracy as interpreted in the 20th century is thus seen to be more than a political formula, more than a system of government, more than a social order.

In order, to accomplish the goals, which the democratic institutions keep before it, there are certain requirements to be met for better performance. On the outset is need the unambiguous and consistent community consciousness. What we want and how to attain in the best of the circumstances prevailing must be very clearly imprinted on our minds. If the clear consciousness is lacking, then the chances to fell prey to casteism, lingualism, communalism, and provincialism are quite bright and in such like conditions around to think of sound policies is not in the fitness of the things. Clarity of community consciousness depends on the moral soundness of the society as a whole. Without honesty, honour and integrity of the people of democracy cannot be a success.[35] An effective public opinion, qualitative social conscience and sound general will are also the requirements to make democracy a laudable success. These factors cannot be credited unless and until the people have proper education. Literacy amounts to considerable growth in the general awareness of the society and the awareness resolves so many aspects which would otherwise remain highly complicated. The political masters in democracies must provide opportunities to the masses for free expression of their opinion and free discussion of issues. Furthermore, the atmosphere should be made of the kind in which people feel genuinely interested in public affairs. For the adequate functioning of political democracy, democracy in terms of economic measures is also required. Abundant inequalities of wealth can amount to the undue influence exerted by the rich on the political masters which leads to nothing less than ignoring overall will of the masses.

Popular Sovereignty

Democracy refers to the fact that the effective political power is with the people. The word democracy has been used ever since the time of Herodotus to devote the form of government in which the ruling power of a state is legally vested, not in any particular class or classes, but in the members of the community as a whole. One of the oldest classifications of governing has been given by Aristotle. As per him, the first type was one which was based on the number of people who run the governments—whether the number is one, few, or many, whereas according to second classification, it was to be noticed whether those in authority use their power for their selfish ends or for the welfare of all. The later classification reveals the ends of the system. When the authority is exercised for the community welfare as a whole, it is called normal or pure, and when it is used to achieve selfish ends, the form of government becomes impure or perverted. Aristotle termed Monarchy, Aristocracy and polity as the pure form of governments, and corresponding to these are tyranny, oligarchy, and democracy, as impure and perverted forms of government. Aristotle's typology of rule depicts democracy as good or bad depending upon the masters ruling.

The principle of popular sovereignty has been expanded by populism, whereby it has encouraged direct and complete translation of popular will into public policy. Further the principle of popular sovereignty has been eroded with the indirect democracy coming into being. For keeping intact the significance and utility of the principle of popular sovereignty on which rests the democratic theory, certain devices, like initiative, widening of electorate, responsibility of government to the majority, referendum, recall, short tenures of the government, and frequent elections to the legislatures have been put to effective use in different political systems based on democracy.

If we analyse at length, we come to know that 'rule by many' in indirect democracy means rule by a numerous minority over numerous majority. The rulers are known as 'elites.'[36] We should not infer from here that the sovereignty in such a situation is not with the people, but with the selected few. We have to satisfy ourselves, from all quarters, with the basic fact that the 'selected few' are representatives of the majority, and it is only the majority which has opted them to rule in comparison to others and the rulers will remain at the seats of power only till they have the majority backing, otherwise, at next chance the rulers will be replaced.[37]

Political Equality and Political Freedoms

Political equality is an other conspicuous trait of democracy. The central principle of the democratic theory, that is popular sovereignty, can never be ensured in true letters and spirits unless there is political equality. By political equality is meant equality in voting. We have discussed above that the direct democracy has been replaced in the contemporary period by the indirect democracy. In indirect democracy the popular sovereignty is with the people can remain in existence only when they have been granted with equal rights to vote and the value of the vote is same without any discrimination on the basis of sex, literacy, colour, creed and affluence. Hence, universal suffrage is the elementary characteristic of democracy. Gone are the days when the right to vote used to be only with the selected few in a state.

Political freedoms mean freedoms of speech, press and assembly etc. Political freedoms amount to an opportunity to participate in political activity. Political freedoms provide an opportunity to analyse and thoroughly scrutinise the public policies and bringing alternatives to various policy issues and also to the policy-makers if they are not governing as per the requirements of time, demands, and circumstances. The existence of democracy as a rule depends upon the degree of effectiveness of the political freedoms.

The notions of political equality and political freedoms raise the issue of minority rights vis-a-vis majority rule.[38] Although both are parts of democracy, reconciling them is difficult if not impossible. Some of the political scientists are of the view that the political equality cannot be there unless there is economic equality. We are aware of the fact that economy plays a considerable role in the life of an individual, a group and also a system. All these aspects whether religious, social, or political are very closely related to economics. The thick and strong relationships between economics and politics has been established since quite long. According to Aristotle, private property was stock to inanimate instrument necessary for the state. He pleaded property requirement for providing right to the people to have political participation. It has been maintained that the maintenance and protection of framers of U.S.A. Constitution. Karl Marx also pleaded for the abolition of private property for the attainment of political justice and goals.[39] Of course, Aristotle held the view that private property is required for political participation, but he did not mean that property institution should be given quantitative importance. He termed property and wealth as means to an end and not an end in itself. Marx also was of the view, that the private property should not be there if the political equality is to be achieved. Therefore, to think of political equality with economic parity seems to be an utmost misnomer.

System Capacity

A democratic system is composed of two elements—citizens effectiveness, and system capacity. Citizen effectiveness means citizens acting responsibility and competently fully control the decisions of the polity, and by system capacity is meant the polity having the capacity to respond fully to the collective preferences of its citizens (Dahl, 1974). The basic principle of the democratic theory, that is, the popular sovereignty would not be in active existence unless the citizens in a given environment have real and actual power of electing their representatives in a fair manner and exercising effective control over the policies framed by the governmental institutions. Of course, it is quite a broad aspect and does not prescribe any concrete base on which genuine and impartial election of the true representatives of the people is made. Where are the parameters by which it can be determined that which candidate suits the best or truly represents the masses ? If factors like caste language, of influence are to be considered for it, then the situation would be further deteriorated. Regarding controlling the decisions of the polity by the citizens also, there are no measuring rods to determine its effectiveness. The citizens effectiveness and system capacity are closely interrelated.[40] Without getting appropriate response from the system, the citizens cannot be in a position to exercise their effectiveness. Citizens have to perform the tasks in a given system and for that the capacity of the system to that effect is required upto considerable extent.

Let us suppose that the government has provided free medical assistance to the citizens belonging to weaker sections, but there are no medicines or doctors available. Would the concession then granted to the citizens regarding free medical assistance be of any effective use ? It is ofcourse, not an easy task to define system capacity as such. The capabilities to undertake a kind of assignment various from system to system. Therefore every system has its own capacity. In a specific system, when we talk in terms of its capacity, we cannot bring out clearly as to which issue is more important and which is less for framing policy on it. If the preferences of citizens are kept in view and the system makes itself capacitated to formulate policies on that, even than it would be difficult to make out how many prefer which, because sometimes there can be clash of issues and preferences also. Supposing the government is asking for the citizens preferences on issue X, Y, and Z and ultimately one is to be decided for making policy on it. If 40% of the citizens chose issue X, 30% go in for issue Y, and 25% opt for issue Z, it will mean that issue X has been demanded by more people. But if we make a sum total to preferences far issues Y and Z, it would amount to 60% of the total which is much more than for issue X: What is required to be kept in view is that which system has more capacity to translate demands of the citizens into policies. If system A has the capacity to formulate more policies on the demands of the citizens than system B then certainly system A is more democratic than system B.

Information

In the absence of proper information with the citizens about the political system, the concept of popular sovereignty cannot be effectively put to use. Without adequate information or by having false, misleading and inconsistent information, exercising effective role on the political systems capabilities and capacities by the people is a remote possibility. People must be thoroughly informed about various issues then only they can build up their preferences which are to be put into the process for formulating policies. Not only the citizens are to be informed about the system, but the system also needs to be informed about the peoples demands for making policies. The system receives information that is analysed and reacted to. The changing environment continuously produced new demands, which the system is informed about, and which determine the load that challenges the efficacy of the system. Information concerning the effectiveness of system outputs on the environment is termed 'feedback' and the extent to which the system is able to adjust to feedback information help to determine its effectiveness of a political system. Information gathered from the citizens is stored so that it may be used in making future decisions.

Democratic Political System Expresses

Popular sovereignty, which means effective political power is resting with the people, political equality and political freedoms, whereby all are equal and have certain freedoms to their credit amounting to active participation of the people in the affairs of the political system, system capacity, revealing the capacity of the system in response to the citizens effectiveness, and information, whereby the citizens "have to be adequately informed about the political systems" activities, and also the system to be informed in appropriate manner about the needs and demands of the citizens for translating those into policies.

NON-GOVERNMENTAL POLICY MAKING AGENCIES

The policy making environment, in addition to the governmental actors and agencies like, legislature, executive, administrative agencies, and courts, includes some non-governmental agencies, like political party, interest groups and citizens are also included. These are known as non-governmental agencies, because irrespective of their dominance and importance these do not have the legalised power to formulate policy decisions.

1. *Political Party* : In modern representative democracies, political parties, in one form or another, are omnipresent.[41] Political party is a body of men united for promoting the national interest on some particular principles on which they are all agreed (Burke, 1970). Political parties, it is alleged, are concerned more with power than with policies. A political party normally observes democratic and peaceful measures for gaining power and implementing its line of action for protecting and promoting its specific interests. The political process is integrated, simplified and stabilised by the political parties. They act as a link between the governmental institutions and the citizens.[41] The electorate are educated, instructed, and activated by the political parties. The political parties accomplish the task of political mobilisation, secularisation and recruitment. Political parties play an important role in presenting issues and setting value goals for the society.

There are various opinions about the origin of the parties. Some hold that they are born of the natural contrast between those who cling to the old and those who embrace the new. Others opine that the political parties arise from the pugnacious instinct of man. There is a conflict of wills in society, and that conflict is decided by the decision of the intermediate mass which is not firmly convinced of the truth of any general cause. To attract its support, it is necessary to advertise one's views. Parties are the natural method of effecting that end. Obviously, the political parties have different programmes and appeal to different sections of society. In India we witness the multi-party system. Political parties are the one which place certain issues before the masses. The political parties normally have programme similar to each other on issues pertaining to social-welfare, public sector, agricultural production, education, better economic measures etc. More often, the political parties perform the task of aggregating the interests, commonly known as interest aggregation, whereby the political parties attempt to translate demands of individuals and interest groups into general policy alternatives.[42] The role played by the political parties in aggregating the interests differ from system to system. For example, in political system where there is single-party system probably no much important role in aggregating the interests is played by the political party. Where the Bi-party system operates, there the parties have to keenly chalkout the issues to be placed before the masses for amassing their support. All those demands which have the support of the majority in the society have to be included. In multi-party system, the political parties approach and appeal on comparatively narrow issues and interests. Of course, in single-party systems, like U.S.S.R. and people's Republic of China, the political party is the important and rather only force in policy-making.

2. *Interest Groups* : These are organised groups in which members share common views and objectives and actively carry on programmes to influence government institutions, officials and policies. Unlike political parties, which seek to win control of and operate the government, interest groups are mainly interested in influencing the determination of public policies that directly or indirectly affect their member's interests. Such groups vary considerably in size, wealth, power, and objectives. Their methods however, are quite similar and include lobbying, electioneering, and propagandising to influence public opinion. Interest groups seek to influence decisions in the legislative, executive and judicial branches.[43]

Groups are naturally the first type of structure which we encounter in the analysis of political system. Interest Groups occupy a place of significance in the process of policy-making in political systems. These play an important role in every political set-up. To understand the working of the political system from close angle, it would be in the fitness of the things to mention the features of the interest groups for being aware of their operational areas and various dimensions. For the attainment of a common goal, individuals form a group. The age at present is an age of competition.[44] For getting the desired ends attained, obviously the members of the group cannot, by any means, take the things in a non-serious or light-manner. They require to actively make efforts in the direction they have kept before them. This amounts to the strong organisational base of the interest groups. Interest groups do not prefer to be politically branded.[45] The major reason for it being that they have to protect and promote their interests whether party 'A' is in power, or party 'B' is in power. Therefore, they very much opt for being non-political entities and keep on playing their game behind the scene only. They are interested only in the protection and upgradation of their aims and views. On the basis of it, the interest groups either have long term objectives or short term objectives. The ones with long term objectives are called political groups, and those having short-term objectives and plans are termed as cause groups, which are formed for the attainment of a specific cause confronting the group members.

Analysed from a broader angle, the interest groups can be divided as

1. Institutional groups—for keeping governmental process in working and performing functions to that effect.
2. Non-Associational groups—formed on the basis of class kinship, religion and relying upon informal, and intermittent communication.
3. Anomic groups—Coming to the scene owing to sudden activities, like processions, strikes, demonstrations, etc.
4. Associational groups—formed for the protection of specific interests of a particular group of individuals.

Interest groups have an important and significant role to play in the policy-making process in almost every type of political system. Of course, their operational capacities vary depending upon the type of political system and its environment.[45] For example, in U.S.A., where there is presidential form of government, and as per constitution the theory of separation of powers is in existence, the operational areas of the interest groups are initially the executive, that is, the president, because he is considered to be all powerful in getting the policies formulated by the Congress. But when the groups feel that they are unable to exercise influence upon the president for the attainment of their goals, the are of operation shifts from the president to the Congress, that is, the legislature. Owing to the lobbying done by various groups, sometimes there are deadlocks between the Executive and the Legislature. Still, if the groups feel that their point of view has not been carried out absolutely or properly, the area is shifted from the legislature to the judiciary. American judiciary is known for its powers and jurisdiction all over the world. Here an attempt of the groups remains to get the policies, formulated by the Congress, hampering their interests being declared null and void.

Interest groups do not get same liberties to operate in Britain. The major reason being that because of the Bi-party system, the political party coming to power attempts to translate the issues, raised by them at the time of elections into policies. Certainly it does not mean that the interest groups are not having any significant role in Britain. There is a marked difference in the role played by political parties and interests groups in Britain.

Interest groups articulate political demands in the society, seek support for these demands among other groups by advocacy and bargaining and attempt to transform these demands into authoritative public policy by influencing the choice of political personnel, and the various processes of public policy-making and enforcement. Political parties tend to free of ideological rigidity, and are aggressive, that is, seek to form the largest possible interest group coalitions by offering acceptable choices of political personnel and public policy. Both interest group system and the party systems are differentiated, bureaucratised and autonomous.[46] Each unit in the party and interest group system comes into the market, so to speak, with an adjusting bargaining ethos. Furthermore the party system stands between the interest group system and the authoritative policy-making agencies and screens them from the particularistic and disintegrative impact of special interests. The party system aggregates interests and transforms them into relatively small number of alternative general policies. Thus, this set of relationships between the party system and the interest group system enables choice among general policies to take place in the cabinet and parliament, and assures that the bureaucracy will tend to function as a neutral instrument of the political agencies (Almond, 1958).

In the totalitarian political systems also interest groups do play some role. Of course, they do not have as free hand and liberties to their credit, to mould the things in the manner suiting their self-interests, as they have in the democratic political set-ups.[47] The interest groups in totalitarian regimes tend not to be absolutely independent. They act merely as an instrument of the state for securing ends which are state determined, or they may become part of the fecade of government for legitimising decisions (Holtzman, 1966). The interest groups are in existence in developing countries as well but are comparatively less organised and effective. At times of crisis the armed forces take up the rule, thus giving an end to the existence of interest groups in some of the developing societies. In such situations the interest groups are made powerless to move because of their lack of organisation and discipline.

Irrespective of the kind of political system—whether presidential democracy, parliamentary democracy, totalitarian, or military rule—the important functions performed by the interest groups is that of articulation of demands. The interest groups articulate the demands in such a manner whereby they could get maximum benefits and can make the governmental agencies to formulate policies suiting their ends. While articulating the demands, the interest groups attempt to provide different policy alternatives to the agencies on which they are exercising their influence. They do not want to loose the game, hence all the information pertaining to the policy issue and possible consequences of the policy are supplied by them to the policy formulators. It has been said that politics rests ultimately upon the conflict and accommodation of interests, brought into being by the manifold inequalities of a society. Broadly speaking, political decision will follow the course along which it is led by the relative strength of interests (Miller, 1962).

Interest Group Techniques

Individual interest groups generally function in a pragmatic and opportunistic fashion, using any method or technique which they believe will serve their purpose effectively. The techniques and tactics which they particular group employs will be determined largely by such factors as size and geographical distribution of the member ship, cohesion of membership, financial resources, prestige, position of the organisation quality of leadership and staff, and relations with the political parties and other interest groups (Turner, 1968). For the attainment of the interests of their groups, the interest groups adopt one technique or the other fort exercising pressure over the policy-makers. The interest groups promote their points of view, defend those, inform about it and various other alternatives, educate or build up the opinion, and even threaten the policy makers through different techniques. The methods or techniques, used by the interest groups vary from country to country depending upon the environment of the system, constitutional authority, social and economic conditions, and strength of the groups etc., are as follows.

Lobbying

In its original meaning lobbying is referred to the efforts of the individuals to influence the votes of legislators, generally in the lobby outside the legislative chamber. In its broadest modern sense, it means any attempt by individuals or groups to influence the decisions of government. It is the most commonly associated with the activities of private interest groups although even public officials may be said to lobby when they attempt to influence the making of public policy by other officials (Encyclopaedia Britannica, 1973). Viewed from a narrower angle, lobbying means an attempt by the organised interest groups over the legislators for the protection and promotion of the interest groups ends. Analysing from a broader point of view, lobbying connotes the influence exercised by the interest groups on all the governmental agencies and actors for the accomplishment of their goals. Hence, lobbying is a technique whereby the government is influenced.[48] In the narrower sense, lobbying is a technique to influence the legislators, this is done through personal meetings, telephone calls, writing of letters, sending delegations and deputations and to the members of the legislature, demonstrating etc. Of course, lobbying is also done in an indirect manner. The political parties field their candidates at the time of elections. These candidates are supported in the elections by organised groups both by men power and material resources. When the candidates supported by the organised groups go to the legislature, they feel it obligatory on their parts upto some extent to protect the interests of those who have helped them. On the basis of the support rendered to the candidates at the time of elections, the interest groups virtually attempt to purchase the legislators and the legislators are, in a way, in the pockets of the interest groups.

Lobbying as a technique of exerting control on policy making agencies differ from country to country. In U.S.A. lobbying is at its peak. It has got the legal sanction behind it. In U.S.A. lobbyist is a person usually acting as an agent for an interest group. He seeks to bring about the passage or defeat of legislative bills or to influence their contents. Lobbyists, often called the third house of the Congress are experts who testify before committees and present important facts on legislative proposals to support their clients interests. Lobbyists are also active in trying to influence decisions made by executive officials and administrators.

In Britain, the lobbying is not that much powerful as it is in U.S.A. It does not play its role openly because of the strong cabinet system and a great degree of organisation discipline of both the political parties. The conservative attitude of the

Britishers is also an important factor for the unpopularity of lobbying.[49] The lobbying is in existence in Britain not because of the statute of parliament, but because of the conventions.

These days the Executive is more powerful. The lobbying as a technique is used by the interest groups for influencing the executive. The executive is having an important place both in the policy-making and policy-implementation. Various committees and commissions appointed by the government, to advise the executive on policy-making issues and policy implementation programmes, become the channels for exercising influence on the executive by interest groups through lobbying. The lobbyists do not hesitate to play their game in the judicial organ of the government also. As the judiciary members are not easy to approach, therefore, lobbying as a technique is put to use there by building public opinion on particular issues and attempting to influence the judiciary.

Strike

Another method or technique which is used by the interest groups for the attainment of their interests is strike. This is a pressure tactic with them for getting their demands accepted.

A strike is a temporary stoppage of work for specific reasons entered into with the expectation that the work will be resumed when a settlement of the grievances is effected. So far as the intentions and attitudes of the strike are concerned they look upon themselves as continuing to retain the status of the employees and of the company against which they are striking, with vested interests in their individual jobs and with the right to return to their jobs when they have reached a mutual agreement over the matters in dispute, or if unsuccessful, when they are willing to return to work on the terms offered by the employer (Peterson, 1963). Of course, the views given by peterson regarding strike concern industrial affairs, but can be applicable to strike in other areas also. Strike as a technique used by interest groups appears to be of a crude type.[50] It is used for getting the demands conceded by the government agencies. The strike is commonly used to effect economic pressure, and is intended to hurt business or to sustain relationships so that normal functions are brought to a halt, or at least inhibited. Normal functioning cannot be resumed until policy changes are instituted. The process of strikes or passive resistance in its most common forms amounts to the intense fixation of pressure or the shifting of the points of attack until a settlement is reached through consultation or capitulation or through compromise (Bondurant). The other techniques used by the interests groups are Bandh and Gherao. These techniques also have been developed by the interest groups for achieving their ends.

3. *Citizen* : The government is supposed to work on the lines whereby it could get maximum gains to the citizens. Of course, the gains and the benefits could be accrued depending upon the resources and capacities of the system. The point of concern over here is not to measure the positive or negative gains or losses the political system has given to its citizens, but to ponder over the importance and significance attached to a citizen so far as his participation in the policy-making process is concerned. We are aware the policies are meant for the public and are implemented on them. In the over all environment, citizens occupy a pivotal position. All the aspects relating to politics and policies are circulating around citizens.[51] The citizens alone put a party or executive in ruling form. The place and position of direct democracy has been taken by indirect democracy. So probably it is not feasible or possible to consult each and every citizen on each and every policy issue or alternatives of that. Of course, in some political systems, like Sweeden, the citizens, still vote directly on legislation. But this practice is not in operation in other countries. It does not mean that the governments or policy framers and doing the things which hamper the over all interests of the citizens.

The governmental agencies do make policies on the issues which the political party in power had placed before the citizens at the time of elections and which were approved by the electorate. It is said that at the time of voting, citizens attach little importance to the policy issues raised by the political parties, and the citizens cast votes on the basis of factors like caste, language, money, regionalism, etc. Whatever considerations may be the citizens have elected their representatives, on the basis of it the government has been formed and policies are made. It is agreed that participation is not direct but it is definitely it is an indirect manner. The citizens, those who have intellectual capabilities keep on contributing to the policy process in the shape of providing new ideas and concepts to the policy framers.[52] Certainly, if an individual citizen's involvement and participation in policy-making is in view, it can be said that no government institution or agency can make it possible to get the views of each and every person under the sun.

REFERENCES

1. Pye, Lucian W., "Introduction : Political Culture and Political Development," in Pye and Verba (eds.), Political Culture and Political Development, U.S.A. Princeton University, Press, 1965.
2. Almond, Gabriel A., Powell, G.B., Comparative Politics : A Developmental Approach, Boston, Little Brown, 1966.
3. Beer and Ulam, Patterns of Government, New York, Random House, 1962.
4. Almond, G.A. and Verba Sidney, The Civic Culture, Boston, Little Brown, 1965.
5. A political system is shaped and re-shaped by the cultural factors of the society.
6. Almond, G.A., and Verba Sidney, *op. cit.*, 1965.
7. The political culture is not fixed and stagnant, on the other hand, it is dynamic, flexible and changeable.
8. Davis, Morton R., and Lewis, V.S., Models of Political Systems, Delhi, Vikas, 1971.
9. The people have become voiceless, passive and silent observers of political spectacles. The Hindu, May 1, 2004.
10. Pye, Lucian W., Aspects of Political Development, Boston, Little Brown, 1966.
11. Government assessment exists at all levels—national, state and local.

12. Dye, Thomas R., Politics, Economics and the Public Policy Outcomes in the Fifty States, Chicago, Rand-McNally, 1966.
13. Dror, Yehezkal, Public Policy Re-examined, Scranton, Chandler, 1968.
14. Economic factors are the main source or base of conflict in the political system.
15. A nation is known by the economic strength in the International arena.
16. Food, clothing and shelter are the basic needs, necessities and requirements of men.
17. Aristotle, father of political science said, 'Man is a social animal outside the society he may be a super human (God) and sub-human (beast).
18. Jain R.B., "Legislative Role Differentiation in Contemporary Societies," in Journal of Parliamentary Information, New Delhi, Vol. XXI, No. 3, 1975.
19. Legislature, Executive and Judiciary are the part and parcel of the political system.
20. The legislature is the main forum for the formulation of the plans, programmes and the policies.
21. The cabinet remains in power so long as it enjoys the confidence of the Parliament. The parliament or legislature has the power to cancel the executive by passing a vote of no-confidence.
22. In Communist China Communist Party is all powerful, all in all and Supreme.
23. In India president is only the ceremonial head, the real powers are enjoys by the Prime-Minister and his/her colleagues.
24. Policy Making now-a-days requires the technical skill, expertise and legal competence.
25. In Russia Communist Party is most dominant and its role is found in all the set-up of the society, govt. and administration.
26. Knowledge is power it is said. Knowledge is the base of power.
27. The legislators are the illiterate, ignorant in the legal, administrative and technical fields. Hence, they depends more and more upon the bureaucracy.
28. Lindbloom, Charles E., The Policy Making Process, Englewood Ciffs, Prentice-Hall, 1968.

29. Deway, John, The Public and Its Problem, New York, 1972.
30. Maxey, Political Philosophies, London, 1964.
31. The judiciary in India is empowered to pass the laws made by the legislature as null and void.
32. People are sovereigns, and masters in a democracy.
33. Mayo, Henry, An Introduction to Democratic Theory, New York, 1960.
34. Robert A. Dahl and Tufte, Edward, R., "Further Reflections" on "The Elitist theory of Democracy," American Political Science Review, June, 1966.
35. Democracy cannot be successful without people having certain basic values.
36. The term Elite means 'Chosen few'.
37. In democracy governments can be changed or replaced peacefully.
38. Blondel, J., An Introduction to Comparative Government, London, Weidenfield and Nicholson, 1969.
39. Turner, Henry, A., "How Pressure Groups Operate" in The Annals of the American Academy of Political and Social Science, Philadelphia, Vol. 319, 1968.
40. "Pressure Groups and Parties in Britain," in American Political Science Review, 1956.
41. Political leaders acts as a bridge or link between the government and the governed.
42. Almond, Gabriel A., "A Comparative Study of Interest Groups and the Political Process" in American Political Science Review, 1958.
43. Turner, *op. cit.*
44. Encyclopedia Britannica, Vol. 14, Chicago, Helen Hemingway Benton, 1973.
45. The Political Parties and the Interest Groups are not one and the same. They are separate, independent and autonomous.
46. Quoted by Dalton E. McFarland in Management : Principles and Practices (New York : Macmillan Co. 1964), p. 191.
47. *Ibid.*, p. 122.
48. Paul H. Appleby, Policy Administration (University of Alabama Press, 1949), p. 7.

49. Seckles Hudson, Organisation and Management : Theory and Practice (Washington D. C. The American University Press, 1957), p. 71.
50. Strike is one of the important weapon used by the Interest Groups for redressal of their grievances.
51. Read Charles E. Lindbloom, The Policy-Making Process (Englewood Cliffs N. J. Prentice Hall Inc. 1968).
52. Charles E. Lindbloom, *op. cit.*

4

POLICY FORMULATION

The analysis in the third chapter has made it clear that policies have the bearing of environment in which they are formulated. The politics and policies cannot be divorced or isolated from the environment and it compelling forces.[1] Policy as a response to environmental challenges varies with the social and physical complexities of the environment. Political as well as environmental pulls and pressures seem necessary to bring about substantial change in policy (Eulan, 1973). It does not seem easy to refer to politics, policy, and environment in a non-serious manner. The environment not only amounts to the pressures for an action by the governmental actors and officials, but also prescribes the political structure through which action is to be taken on the demands and pressures. Of course, there is no unanimity or agreement on the amount of influence exercised by the environmental factors on the policy-formulation, but one thing is clear that the environment does influence the policies, and the policy cannot be separated from the environment.[2] The needs of the society are the determinants of the policies upto great extent.

The stress or the focus in this chapter, would be on the formulation or framing of public policies in a political system, and what are the methods whereby the governmental institutions function to make policies on the demands arising out in the environment, and the legislature reacts with the executive, and bureaucracy, and the executive inter-action with bureaucracy etc.

The system model discussed in chapter I reveals the characteristic features of a system. As per Almond's input-output analysis the process of policy formulation is based on four points, political socialisation and recruitment, Interest aggregation, Interest articulation, and political communication.

Depending upon it, the system's outputs have been listed by him as rule making, rule-application, and rule-adjudication. Similarly, the Black-Box model of political system given by Easton speaks of demands and supports becoming decisions and policies through the conversion process and the remaining issues are again fed back through the same procedure. Of course, the system model does not make clear what goes on within the system, or in other words, what is there in the little black-box of Easton through which the issues and problems are translated into policies.

Obviously, the policies which are made by the governmental agencies and institutions are based on certain policy issues and problems. Normally, a very less attention and significance is attached to identify the policy problems. Without taking into consideration the policy problems, perhaps the policy analysis will remain incomplete. The policy process is based on the determination of policy problems. Likewise, the final evaluation to measure the outcome and impact of policy cannot be made adequately without knowing the basic problems on which the policy was formulated.

Identifying Policy Problems : Government in political system is meant to case for all the aspects concerning the life of the individuals. Whether the issue is social, economic, religious law and order, security measures, fundamental rights, or anything else, it is obligatory or compulsory on the part of the government to do maximum for its inhabitants. We are living in the welfare state, therefore, any problem amounting to tension anxiety and disturbance to the people and for which they want such measures from the government in the shape of policy can be broadly known as policy problem. The question arises over here is, do all the problems faced by the people in the political system, are the policy problems ? The answer to this is that only those issues on which people want some action in the form of policy are considered policy problems. If we do not go to the court against action 'X' how can be expect the court to sort out the things for us pertaining to action 'X'. It is said that the mother also does not feed the baby unless he cries.[3] Therefore, when we reconcile to poor standards of education and do not make any effort to move government to adopt policies for improving the education standards, the government cannot be blamed for it. At some occasions, the alarm for seeking governments action to a particular effect is raised by those who are not directly affected by that. For example, if the opposition leaders in a given political system want the government to provide more job avenues to the people, it does not mean that the leaders want jobs for themselves, but they are pleading the cause of the common public.

The problems and aspirations are such which every man is having. Does it mean that the problem of Mr. A, who is a post-graduate, regarding not getting suitable job according to his educational qualification is a public problem and the government is required to formulate some policy on it whereby Mr. A could get a job ? To this 'No' is the answer. But if a considerable educated youth are not in position in get jobs, then certainly the government has to think on the lines whereby such avenues are opened because of which the educated youth could get jobs and they do not become frustrated and rebellious. The public problems are those which have a broad effect and these not only include those who are directly affected but also all those who are indirectly affected.[4] Keeping the broad base and effect of a problem in view, we term it as a public problem. Supposing the person has been robbed of his belongings and he goes to the police station for seeking help of the police. But the police does not pay any heed to his requests. He approaches some influential person of the area and through his influence exercised on the police is able to get the robbers traced and his belongings back. Uptil this it was a problem of purely private nature and gets finished with the man going back to his place with his belongings. Let us suppose that on getting cold response from the police, the person, instead of approaching the influential person, publicises the issue and tries to get other persons, having suffered by the irresponsible behaviour of the police, on one platform and then they all collectively raise their voice and pressurise the legislators and government officials in recognising the problem for making policy on the problem will then become public from private.

Problems are of various kinds. It can be divided into three broad types—Distributive, Redistributive, and Regulatory (Lowi, 1964). Distributive problems of small number of persons and can be taken up for consideration one by one. Redistributive problems seek transfer of resources among large groups in society, regulatory problems are those which ask for the curtailment of activities or limitation of the actions of the others. Problems are also distinguished as Basic and Routine. Basic problems are those on which the community as a whole and the governmental officials feel concerned and go in for the formulation of a policy, and Routine problems are those which concern the way government is organised, and the manner in which it operates and performs functions. Another distinction about the problems can be made as National Problems and International Problems. National Problems include all the problems pertaining to agriculture, food storage, education, population growth, inflation, education social-welfare, law and order etc. Within the system, the International problems include the attitude of foreign countries towards the system, trade with other countries, etc. Policy Problems and Public Opinion. Public Opinion is the beliefs and attitudes of people on an issue. It may relate to matters of fact or matter of preference. An opinion expressing preference can be classified in terms of its direction and its intensity. Public opinion is not a unified whole, but an aggregate of many, generally diverse, individual opinions. There is no agreed view on the amount of influence the public opinion can exercise in getting a problem identified as a policy problem. Edmund Burke, British political philosopher and a conservative, held the view that the elected representatives in democracies are meant to care for the interests of their electorate, but this does not mean that they should necessarily act in accordance to their wishes so far as policy-making is concerned. Some of the theorists are of the view that the most straight forward, democratic manner for making public policy would be for policy makers to follow public opinion. It is rather difficult to resolve the issue whether public opinion should be taken into consideration by the policy formulators or not. But even this is not easy to analyse whether public opinion has some influence over policy makers or not. It is complicated and complex issue—who influences whom ? Whether the public opinion exercise its influence over policy makers, or the policy makers mould public opinion to their ends is very difficult to analyse.

According to key, Government as we have seen attempts to mould public opinion towards support of the programmes and policies it espouses. Discussion of public opinion often loses persuasiveness as it deals with the critical question of how public opinion and government actions are linked. The democratic theorist found his doctrines on the assumption that an interplay occurs between mass opinion and government. When he seeks to delineate that interaction and to demonstrate the precise bearing of the opinions of private citizens on official decision, he encounters almost insurmountable obstacles. In despair he may conclude that the proposition that public opinion enjoys weight in public decision is a myth and nothing more, albeit a myth that strengthens a regime so long as people believe it (Key, 1967). Key made an effort to emphasise that public opinion has its effect on public policy and the communication channels from masses to the policy-formulators are elections, political parties and interest groups.[5] One does not come across qualitative and substantial material to the effect to support that public policy is influenced by public opinion. It would not be wrong to say that it is the public policy which influences the public opinion and not the public opinion affects the public policy.

We are residing in an economic age.[6] Most of the human beings are involved in their personal affairs. Neither the majority of them have the time, awareness and interests to the aware of all the issues which the policy formulators have before them for making policies on. Moreover, how the public opinion can effectively affect decision makers, when the memories of the public are so short.[7] One seldom finds consistency prevailing in the minds of the masses over some issues. When the electorate opposed the excesses committed by Congress–I during internal emergency in India between June 1975 to early 1977, they defeated the party in March 1977 Lok Sabha elections. And Janata Party came in to power. But due to the internal quarrels and conflicts it lost power in 1980 general election. What made the electorate to vote for the Congress-I again in January 1980 elections, to a considerable majority. The public opinion is quite inconsistent and unstable.[8] Furthermore, the policy formulators rarely receive the true version of the views and attitudes of the public in general. The decision-makers rarely get chance to openly discuss the things with commoners on policy issues. The information received by the policy makers is through newspapers, interest groups etc. and not by the common persons.

Most of the individuals make their opinions on the basis of some information or the other received by them, in a short-cut, easy and convenient method. They depend mostly on Newspapers. And whatever views are listed there, are normally adopted by the individuals. The major cause for this is that neither the common citizen has adequate knowledge or information, nor analytical power to assess a policy issue and formulate opinion on it. The newspapers and magazines mould the public opinion to a greater extent.

What to talk of under-developed or developing societies, even in the developed societies, only a very marginal section of the society takes the initiative of expressing its opinions on policy issues and public policies to the policy-makers. The majority of the people are of the view that the government has its own way to decide the issues and their opinion or views will not be taken into consideration. Moreover, there are no adequate platforms or channels at which and through which the common people are in position to communicate and express their opinion. In the light of the authoritative allocation of values and the legal sanction behind the governmental decisions, people feel scared also in expressing their views against the policy issue taken up or policy formulated by the governmental agencies. Studying the interaction between congressional voting and public opinion in U.S.A. on policy issues, Miller and Stokes found low correlations between the voting records of Congressmen and the attitudes of their constituents on social welfare issues, and even lower correlation on foreign policy issues (Miller and Stokes, 1963).

It does not mean that public opinion has nothing to do with the identification on policy issues and problems. If the public opinion is not directly exercising its influence on policy issues determination, it is certainly doing so in an indirect manner. If we probe into the constituents of government agencies identifying policy problems and formulating policies on those, we find the representatives of the common people over there. These representatives have to take into consideration the demands and needs of their electorate and moreover, the political parties—both in ruling and opposition—have to keep in view the requirements of their voters, for the very simple reason that they have to contest again and for that have to seek the support of the public. An issue posing challenge to a sizeable number of people has to be taken up by the government to make policy on.

Policy Problems and Elites

We have discussed already about the role of elite and policy in chapter II. It has been made clear through the analysis in the preceding paragraphs that public opinion or more relevantly called 'mass opinion' does not have any direct influence over the government for identifying policy issues as problems for formulating policies on these. Moreover, specifically, we can say that it is the elite opinion which does help in determining problems for making policies. While determining the impact and influence of popular preferences on public policy, Key has said that it is the "thin stratum of persons referred to variously as the political elite, the political activities, or influencials who matter in the identification of policy problems.[9]

If at all there is need to take opinion or to know the preferences of people on some issues for determining policy problems by the government, the certainly it is the elite preference which is kept in view more forcefully in comparison to the mass opinion or preferences. It does not lead to the point that the policies are determined by the preferences and opinion of the elite only. In order to make some mass base for the policies formulated by the government, the elites in the environment are consulted and taken into confidence.[10] Sometimes the elites are in a position to get their demands termed as policy problems because of the various pressures adopted by these influential interest groups. Moreover, the elites are educated and cultured, and have capability to understand better than the common masses, and have status and position in society, therefore, they can understand the government policies or the issues identified by the government as problems for policy-making in a comparatively better manner than ordinary citizens. We have referred to earlier in this chapter that a demand becomes public only when it is supported by a sizeable number of people.

Obviously, the elites have the capacity to amass support for issues confronting them. It is a general phenomenon that if their are two individuals A and B, A is the one who has status, position, and affluence to his credit, and B is just an ordinary man. Most of the people will side with the issue raised by A and very few will standby B, because of the factor that B is not that influential as A is. Hence, the elites in the society can certainly make base among the people for their demands and problems. The concentration of power in the elites is because of the fact that the numerous people in the system are lazy, indifferent, and politically neutral. They neither have the time, nor the resources or interest to analyse the issues being taken up for making policies.

Identifying Policy Agenda

Agenda is a list of specific items of business to be considered at a legislative session or at a conference of meeting. The question over here is to know what is the criterion for making an issue or problem on the agenda for making policy on it. Why issue or problem 'K' has been taken up and why problem 'D' has been left out of the agenda. The citizens are faced with hundreds of problems individually and collectively. Why all these problems are not kept on the agenda for making policies ? The governmental institutions engaged in policy making select only a few of the issues causing tension and anxiety among the masses. The demands and the issues chosen by the government make the policy agenda. Policy agenda is always brief in comparison to policy demands and one can easily make a distinction between the two. Demands or problems are the ones which people want to achieve or get rid of, whereas the agenda is the one which the government in power decides for making policies. Some confuse policy agenda with the priorities of the party in power. They feel that the party who has won in the elections will try to translate the issues raised by it in its election manifesto into policies. The priorities of the party do not always find place in the agenda in a ranking order because there are sometimes more compelling situations, demands, and issues which need immediate action by the government.

Identification of the problems and prescription of alternative solutions to it occupies an important place in the policy formulation process. For providing better means to the people or to cope with the challenges arising out of various problems confronting the citizens and demands being supported for governmental action on the issues causing problems to the society get a place on the agenda of the policy formulators. When a problem is faced by the society and various alternatives are suggested, it becomes a policy problems and the policy formulators are compelled to take action on that. The view is held by some that in an open system, where the government is of the people and by the people. But in reality the things are not as we think in an ideal manner. Unless and until the issue on which policy is required is emphatically publicised, and governmental agencies at various levels pressurised, the issue will never find place on the agenda of policy-making. The important agencies normally engaged in publicising the issues and pressurising the government are political parties, interest groups, influential citizens etc. It does not mean that only those issues are placed on the agenda which have been backed by some groups and for which the government has been pressurised. Keeping in view, the priorities and the requirements of the system, the government placed the issues on agenda whereby it could mean some meaningful business for the overall betterment of the country from so many spheres and angles.

The leadership in a system plays an important role in agenda setting. If the presidential system in democracy is taken in consideration, then it is the president and his team which make the agenda. If on the other hand, parliamentary democracy is in view, then it is the Prime-Minister and his Cabinet which make the agenda. Public policy has been defined as 'whatever government chooses to do or not to do". Therefore, the role of the executive in agenda setting cannot be minimised. The executives normally do it for attaining political gains in the times to come, because through policies they can please the masses and can get their support in the ensuring elections. Sometimes the sudden incidents also compel the government to bring an issue on the agenda. The mass media also helps in getting an issue on the agenda. The wider coverage given to problem in the various newspapers can make the government seriously think about the issue, because otherwise it can turn the mass-opinion against the government. A two-fold classification of agendas has been made by Cobb and Elder (1972), that is, systemic agenda, and institutional, or governmental agenda. The systemic agenda consists of all issues that are commonly perceived by members of the political community as meriting public attention and involving matters within the legitimate jurisdiction of existing governmental authority (Cobb and Elder, 1972). It consists of normally the issues requiring governmental action on a problem to be dealt with authoritatively to resolve the same. The systemic agenda will be in existence at every level-local, state, and national, in a system. To better the ties of relationships with Pakistan may be only on the national systemic agenda, whereas to deal with the law and order, problem may find place on all the local, state, and national agenda. Institutional agenda is of more specific and basic nature in comparison to systemic agenda. It consists of the problems which are of great importance. Hence, it requires serious thought over and minute consideration of the policy-makers.

The issues in institutional agenda can be divided into two parts—new issues and old issues. New issues are the ones which emerge all of a sudden and cause great anxiety among the masses—For example, to deal with the nation-wide strike by the Railway men, or to deal with the riots took place after the assassination of Prime Minister Mrs. Indira Gandhi, or the gas leakage amounting to death of so many persons in Bhopal in 1984, etc. The old issues are the ones with which the public officials and governmental agencies are very well aware of. For example, the additional dearness allowance, interim relief to certain categories of employees, providing better security measures etc. It is said that old issues tend to receive priority from decision makers, who constantly find their time if limited and that their agenda is loaded. Decision makers presume that older problems warrant more attention because of their longevity and the greater familiarity officials have with them. (Cobb and Elders 1972). However, there does not seem to be much force in the view of Cobb and Elder that because of the familiarity of the public officials and the old issues take more attention or because of issues remaining pending for a long time the decision makers attach more importance to it. The issues which crop up suddenly definitely require thorough and detailed attention of the decision-makers because they are new to the problems and obviously need to ponder over those more keenly and minutely.

Thomas R. Dye has defined public policy as whatever governments choose to do or not to do. Note that we are focusing not only on government action, but also on government in action, that is, what government chooses not to do. We contend that government inaction can have just as great impact on society as government action (Dye, 1975). An analysis has been made above as a how various problems find place on the policy agenda. It is equally noteworthy to point out that what are the forces and factors which make policy-makers not to include various items on the policy agenda. In a similar manner, when an issue which would hamper the interests of the influential individual when it will take shape of a policy, which be torpedeed to their best right in the beginning so that the issue may not catch public attention. At the time of elections man power and money power plays a very important role, the elites and the elected members frames the policy so as to suit their helpers, supporters and well-wishers.[12]

Sometimes the onus for non-decision making lies on the political system itself. The normal functioning of every political system is to resolve certain issues and to create obstacles for resolving others. It does not mean that the governmental institutions do not intend to solve all the problems. They try to encash upon the issues which they have resolved and wait for greater rewards to solve certain issues after sometime. The Congress-I government headed by Prime Minister Mrs. Indira Gandhi did not solve the Punjab and Assam issues. But the new government under the Prime-Ministership of Mr. Rajiv Gandhi solved these problems shortly after being in the saddle of power. The crucial problem in politics is the management of conflict.[13] No regime could endure that did not cope with the problem. All politics all leadership, all organisation involves the management of conflict. All conflict allocates space in the political universe. The consequences of conflict are so important that it is inconceivable that any regime would survive without making on attempt to shape the system. All forms of political organistions have a bias in favour of the exploitation of some kinds of conflicts and the suppression of others because organisation is the mobilisation of bias. Some issues are organised into politics, while others are organised out (Schattschneider, 1961).

If such is the case, then who is ultimately responsible and empowered to make agenda ? Who has to take the decision on what is to be decided ? Obviously, the government institutions frame the policy agenda in the light of welfare programmes, certain compelling circumstances, and to meet the demands supported by the masses, the issues are listed on the agenda for policy formulation. The mass media plays an important role in mobilizing mass opinion in favour of or against certain issues.[14] The newspapers, magazines and journals etc. also give coverage to the issues raised by government depending upon the nature and style of functioning of the reporting agency. There are certain newspapers which always write for or against the government. The Television, Radio, and Press are supposed to provide accurate picture to the masses so that their reactions could be known genuinely. The governmental authorities should not exercise authority on forcing the news media to present distorted pictures favouring the rulers. The ultimate power and authority to place issues on agenda or formulating policy-agenda is with the governmental actors and agencies. Of course, sometimes, the non-governmental agencies and actors like interest groups, media sources, opposition leaders and other influential individuals can make an issues entry into agenda. But in such cases also, the issue would be placed on agenda for active consideration by the governmental agencies only.

Policy Proposals : The policy issues and problems which would find place on the policy agenda are known as policy proposals on which the action would be taken for translating the same into public policies meant to attain some goals or to accomplish some tasks. However, it does not necessarily mean that whatever the proposals are, all are going to be converted into policies. Here also it depends on the 'real-masters' to decide whether they want to take some concrete action on the policy proposal or not. Sometimes hesitatingly, the policy issue is given the status of policy proposal by putting it on agenda under compulsions on the government being exercised by the influential interest groups or elites in the system. We have discussed above also that the public policy is whatever government chooses to do or not to do. Hence, it cannot be categorically stated that every policy proposal is definitely going to be a public policy.

In a dictatorial and totalitarian political systems, the Heads of the States are the ones to take initiative on developing policy proposals. Even in the democracies, it is now expected by the legislatures that the executive heads will float the policy proposals before them. In a parliamentary form of democracy such as that of India, it is the Prime Minister and his cabinet who bring the policy proposals to the parliament for enacting policies on those. And in the presidential form of democracy, like that of U.S.A. the Congress expects the President and his advisors to bring the proposals to it. Obviously, on the face of it, this does not mean that whatever proposals the political executive will bring to the legislature, they are bound to be passed and enacted. The legislatures also put its foot down on certain issues and in such cases the executives have to mould the proposals in the light of the discussions made in the legislatures. The querry arises over here is whether the political executive is virtually that competent to develop proposals in an absolutely fool-proof manner. Of course, the political executive has to depend upon the various administrative agencies and experienced governmental officials for developing the proposals and for feeding relevant data to the political executive for presenting the proposals to the legislature in a well-to-do-shape. The various government departments have systematic material pertaining to their fields with them. Moreover, in comparison to the political executives, the departmental officials have more expertise to their credit, on the basis of which they are more capacitated to draft the policy proposals. It does not mean that the political, executive has no hand in the drafting and development of policy proposals and all is done the governmental officials and administrators.

The proposals and broad guidelines are, in most of the cases, given by the political executive only. The administrative agencies simply assist the executive in preparing the blue-print of the policy proposals. In some cases, certain policy proposals are suggested to the political executive by the administrative agencies, but it must be noted that these are always in suggestive forms and the final wish to bring it to the legislature or get policy made on these proposals is always that of the executive. Other than the various administrative agencies, certain commissions and advisory groups are created by the political executive to develop proposals for policies. The appointment of Sarkaria Commission by the Government of India to make suggestions of the Centre-State relations, and the Bains Commission appointed by the Government of Punjab to recommend the release of persons arrested during August 1981 to July 1985 on the charges of terrorist activities, the Mathew Commission to settle the areas to be given to Haryana in Lieu of Chandigarh's transfer to Punjab, and the Economic Advisory council to advise the Prime Minister reconstituted in December 1985 are few of the examples of commissions and councils made by the government to assist, suggest, and advise the political executive on various policy proposals. There are so many instances when the governments had formulated policies on the proposals developed by the commissions and councils.

The role of legislatures cannot also be minimised in bringing policy proposals for action. The legislators are the representatives of the masses.[15] They are more aware and conscious of the demands, needs and problems of their constituencies. Moreover, they have to watch the interests of those on whose help they have been in position to be in the legislature. They keep on bringing policy problems and issues before the political executive in writing, in personal meetings with the political executives, and through discussions in the House, for getting the issues and problems listed on the policy agenda and make those as policy proposals amounting to action in the form of public policy enacted. The interest groups also exercise their influence in getting the policy proposals formulated. They do not leave any chance and, therefore, approach both the executive officials and legislators for such an action which suit them for the attainment of their self-interests. We have discussed earlier also that it is not possible for the political executive and legislators to ignore the demands made by the interest groups. It does not mean that whatever the interest groups want they are able to achieve, but certainly it would not be wrong to say that they achieve success in getting some of their problems on the policy agenda for their becoming policy proposals and ultimately being enacted as public policies.

Policy Formulation

Getting a policy problem translated into public policy, there are various governmental actors and agencies involve of course, non-governmental actors and agencies are also in the picture through comparatively less significantly. But in the whole of the process there are three organs which occupy a prominent place in the policy formulation. These are—Legislature, Executive and Bureaucracy. First of all let us examine their interaction with each other in formulating policies.

1. *Legislature-Executive Interaction* : Legislature and the executive are the two most important organs which play a significant part or role in formulating the policies. Speaking in terms of the major power of running the government and public affairs should rest with the duly elected representatives of the people, this is, with the legislature.[16] But in recent times the legislature is viewed from the executive angle. The executive is the initiator of most of the policy proposals in the legislature for formulation of policies on those. It is somewhat justified also on the part of the executive to have amassed this power of initiation or making policy proposals and placing those before the legislature. The overall responsibility of the state administration is that of the executive, which is composed of the members of the legislature, normally belonging to the

majority party or parties, and is responsible to the legislature.[17] In the light of it a considerable emphasis has been laid on the executive's role in policy formulation because it is strongly felt that the executive has more adequate knowledge and information about various policy issues and demands. The role of the legislature is only to help the executive in carrying out its policies. Certainly it does not amount to the point that the legislature has no power at all and it is simply to ratify the issues and proposals laid down by the executive before it. Some political scientists are of the view that the legislature has enough information but it cannot process it properly. Still so many instances can be quoted when the legislature has turned down the proposals of the executive. We do not aim to analyse the relationship between the both on negative lines or to determine which is more supreme. The executive is a part and parcel of the legislature.[18] The executive heads are also being elected by the people and so feel their responsibility equally alongwith that of the legislators towards the masses and the means to be adopted in the shape of policies for providing relief to them or for meeting with their demands. The executive has full fledged government departments and organisations at its disposal for assisting it in preparing the drafts and suggesting various alternatives to the proposals. The executive only initiates the proposals and it is for the legislature whether to ratify the same or not.[19]

Of course, keeping in view the strength of the party and its organisational discipline, the executive is, in majority of the cases, able to get the proposals ratified by the legislature because the party or parties, the executive hails from has or have majority in the legislature. The legislature has its own procedure for analysing the proposals initiated by the executive. These have to pass through strenuous discussions, debates, and minute scrutiny by the committees of the legislature. Whatever changes or amendments, the legislative feel required are made in the process of enactment of the policy. After doing the same, the proposal now known as policy after being formulated by the legislature and approved by the

Executive Head, again comes to the executive for getting it implemented appropriately. Any lapses in implementation are keenly and forcefully, observed and pointed out by the legislature and the executive has to properly answer the same as it is ultimately responsible to the legislature and can stay in power as long as it enjoys the confidence of the legislature.[20] The legislature also plays its role in making proposals for formulating policies. The legislators meet and discuss the issues with the members of the executive. It is said that all the compromises between the executive and the legislature do not come to surface when the proposal is laid before the House, but these are made at earlier and initial stages where the legislators points of consideration are also accommodated in the policy proposal a such. In situations where the executive does not have absolutely majority in the legislature the executive head makes it a point not to create such kind of situation where his government would be in dilemma, and so he has to accommodate the members of the legislature in getting his point through.

2. *Legislature-Bureaucracy Interaction* : Bureaucracy is an administrative system, especially of governmental agencies, that carries out policy on a day-to-day basis, that uses standardised procedures, and that is carried based on specialisation of duties. It also connotes a system where in excessive growth of administrative agencies is accompanied by concentration of power in administrative officials, excessive red tape, dedication to routine, and resistance to change. The term 'Bureaucracy' is often used simply to designate the administrative or executive branch of government.[21]

The bureaucracy helps and assists the political executive in making the draft of policy proposals which are submitted before the legislature by the executive. In a direct manner, the bureaucracy is not related with the legislature, but in an indirect manner, it has interaction with the legislature through executive. Executive is answerable and responsible to the legislature, whereas the bureaucracy is answerable and questionable to the executive which is directly responsible to the legislature. The bureaucrats are not under the control of legislature. However, the legislature can ask about their functioning from the executive which has control over the bureaucracy. The proposals laid down before the legislature are formulated with thorough assistance of the bureaucracy and when the policy is finally formulated, again it is implemented by the bureaucrats and administrative agencies.

3. *Executive and Bureaucracy* : It has been discussed earlier that the bureaucracy assists the executive in preparing policy proposals and suggesting various alternatives to the executive. In the formulation of policy proposals which are the base of the policies the bureaucracy works with executive in a well planned out and thoughtful manner. The bureaucracy sometimes even convince the executive for the initiation of some policy. The bureaucrats have long experience and expertise to their credit which are put to effective use in assisting the executive in framing policy legislation drafts and also in implementing the policies. Therefore, viewing in broad angle, it becomes evident that the executive is in position to frame policies and implement those with the assistance of the bureaucracy. However, it does not mean that the bureaucracy has predominance over executive in policy formulation. The relationship is some what akin to master-servant relationship. The bureaucracy assists the executives on the lines the executive wants it.

Basically, the formulation of policies is composed of activities of two kinds. Firstly, what is to be done. That means the proper emphasis on the points which are to be dealt within a policy. For example, what type of national education policy India should have where by people could have more Job prospects after attaining educational qualifications. And, secondly, how the policy proposal legislation is to be drafted. in this activity attention is attached to the situational factors so that when adopted, the policy could have bearings and effective outcomes. The major involvement in the first activity is that of political executive. Of course, at some points the legislators also take lead. In the second activity, the bureaucracy which assists the executive in drafting the legislation proposal as well as providing adequate measures for its execution in true letters and spirits.

4. *Policy Decisions* : Policy decisions are the combination of certain basic and routing decisions. Basic decisions are those which amount to significant aspects in a policy, and routine decisions are the ones which amount to day-to-day working for the carrying out of the policy in an effective manner.[22] Policy decision is based on the action of governmental institutions and officials for approving, modifying a rejecting a policy alternative. Policy decision stage in the policy formulation process is ahead of making, selecting among various alternatives. Here the policy formulators have a preferred alternative and they are to make concrete actions for getting the decision made on an alternative selected. During the decision stage, various facts come through. At some, certain issues induced in the proposal of alternative are rejected, some more are added, some modifications are made on certain accounts, the different view points are resolved through bargains and compromises, and the process goes on till the policy deision becomes only a formality waiting to be announced. The major and important actors involved in the policy decisions are the governmental institutions and actors such as the executive, the legislature, the bureaucracy, and the judiciary. However, certain non-governmental actors and institutions also do take part in the policy decision making. In democratic political systems, which are obviously based on the principle of popular sovereignty, the policy decision is made by the duly elected representatives of the people, that is, the legislature. This is what the theory of democracy demands. However, in reality, the major policy decision making is made on the initiative taken by the executive. Though the executive takes the lead in deciding the policy agenda, policy proposals and all pertaining to it, yet the policy decision is finally made by the legislature. Whatever is not approved by the legislature is not considered legitimate and legal by the people.

Decision makers are those who exercise the powers for making and implementing policy decisions. Official decision makers may be influenced, sometimes decisively, by private individuals and groups that serve as consultants or function as unofficial members of the nation's establishment. Elites and general public may also affect policy actions by setting limits on the decision makers through support for some policies and rejection of others. In most of the political systems, the head of the government plays the key role in the decision making process. In others, the highest decision maker may be the leader of the single party that controls power as in many communist political systems. In many democratic systems, key legislators of the majority party in the House also play a role in making policy decisions.

Further, we can view the decision making as an Individual process and as a collective process.[23] The personality, thinking and capabilities of the decision maker is reflected in the decision and rather has a considerable affect on the decision taken. Everybody has a different angle of viewing a thing and situation. His beliefs, attitudes, and values definitely play a considerable part in decision making and on the decisions made. An individual has sometimes a number of forces and factors influencing him at the time of resolving a particular issue or taking decisions. What is the ideology ? What are the demands and problems ? What is the type of situation ? What are the environment compulsions ? etc. All have direct influence on the mind of the decision-maker at the time of taking decision. In democratic political system the decision make has to take considerably in consideration the programme and priorities of the political party he belongs to. In parliamentary democracy, the political party having majority in the House is in position to formulate cabinet. The real executive that is, the Prime Minister at the time of making decisions shall have to keep in view the ideology, programme, and priorities of his party. Moreover, party organisations have discipline and the party man cannot go against the party norms and values. The individual decision maker also have in view the interests of his constituencies. He has been supported by the electorate and the decision maker has to safeguard the interests of his constituencies.

In most of the cases it is not the individual alone who matters through and through for policy decision making. It is group of influential individuals, mostly governmental officials and actors who are involved in decision making. Obviously, every individual has a different angle of thinking and acting in a particular situation. The phenomenon becomes rather complex and complicated because when there are number of individuals involved with different parameters and view points then how the ultimate decisions have to be reached at. There are various styles of decision making in collective process of decision making.

Styles of Decision-Making

There are various styles of decision making in collective process of decision making. Mitchell and Mitchell have described these styles as Bargaining, Competition, Command, Conflict and Cooperation (Mitchell and Mitchell, 1972).

1. *Bargaining* : Since the decision-making is not a job of a single individual and there are various individuals and groups involved in it, and everyone is having his own priorities, therefore, a situation has to brought or point was to be evolved where all share a common platform and support the view in majority. Let us take the example of a parliamentary democratic political system. We know that the party which has the majority of the members in the House will have its government. Suppose the party in government has simple majority in the House and the party leaders have to take note of all the party members in the House on the question of taking policy decision. There are groups in the party, which every political party normally has, and the groups have different priorities before them. Let us assume that there are three groups X, Y and Z and have different priorities. Ultimately, the policy of give and take would be adopted whereby some points of each group would be carried out and some would be rejected through a bargaining. the bargaining is also made when there

is coalition government, or in other situations also when the ruling party has to go alongwith the opposition parties also at some occasions.

2. *Competition* : Through competition also the decisions are made when the various groups have different values and preferences and they are making efforts in getting the decisions made suiting their view points, such a game is known as that of competition among the groups. Supposing out of three groups X, Y and Z 'X' has fixed eyes on getting a policy decision for immediate future, and 'Y' for a policy for distant future and both are racing their horses to achieve their ends. Both the groups have almost equal strength. In such like cases, it would be important to see the decision of group 'Y' as a whole or majority of the members belonging to group 'Y'.

3. *Command* : Through command the differences among various groups are reduced. This is common mainly in totalitarian and dictatorial political system, where one man's word is termed as final and not much significance is attached to others.[24] But now the command is often used in democracies also in deciding the issues. Chief Minister, Haryana wanted the outgoing president of Haryana Pradesh Congress Committee-I to continue, but his opposition group within the Congress I-did not like it, the All India Congress Committee-I gave its command and appointed a new president of H.P.C.C. (I) in 1985. During Mrs. Indira Gandhi's Prime Ministership Mr. Morarji Desai did not like her move on Bank nationalisation and ultimately resigned from the Deputy Prime Ministership and Finance Ministership when his point was not given any attention. Therefore, in democracies also, where right to have one's own view point is almost guaranteed the role of command and resolving the issue by it is often witnessed in the fitness of being able to reach at a decision.

Bargaining, which means, give and take occurs within equals, whereas command is in the relationship of hierarchically superiors with the subordinates. Those who agree or abide with the instructions and command of the superiors are rewarded in the times to come and those who resist it are paid in the same terms in future by the superiors. Whether it is the principle of popular sovereignty or political equality, one has to compromise on the count that principle of in equality prevails in the policy decision making and in the political system even at the top are few with superior position and so[illegible]e with not that superior standing and sound footings.

4. *Conflict* : The settlement over the issues in policy decision making also takes place through conflict. Over here the meaning of the conflict is not coming to the crude and violent of resolving the issues but is by adopting certain such like tools and techniques where one party get capacitated to make other party withdraw. All the actors visibly involved in the decision making process are eager to get the things take place to their own ends and suitability. Of course, own ends does not mean their personal gains or goals attainment but in accordance to their priorities and ideologies. In such like situation, it often happens that there is clash of interests which cannot be resolved other than coming in conflict with each other. When the persuasion, bargaining, and competitive measures fail the conflict emerges.

5. *Co-operation* : Policy decision making process is the one which normally is based on the co-operative efforts of the actors and institutions involved there in. Ultimately, the decision makers role is to formulate a policy.

All the five different decision-making processes or styles discussed above put us in the situation where we cannot prefer any one of these in comparison to others for making policy decision. Infact, all the styles are adopted by the actors simultaneously. At one time an actor or group might bargain with another, in another situation they may be in competition with each other, correspondingly in third situation one may be commanding or being commanded, having conflicts with each other and at end making the decisions co-operatively.

Whatever style is adopted, the policy formulators always have in view that the policy decisions taken by them must by all means justify the decisions being made by them. If the policy decision is not readily accepted by the society, it means the policy makers have failed in their objective. Whether the policy has been made on the initiation of the governmental institutions of their own, on the demand of the interest group, or other associations and the groups in the society, ultimately the policy should speak like serving the interests of the public. The policies formulated must be in accordance to the environment factors in general and cultural factors in particular. The norms, views, beliefs, and attitudes prevailing in the society have to be kept in consideration by the policy decision makers for getting appropriate approval of the public in regard to the acceptance of the policies made.It has been rightly said men in general judge more according to their eyes than their hands, since everyone is in a position to observe, just a few to touch.[25] Everyone sees what you appear to be, few touch what are, and those few do not dare oppose the opinions of the many who have the majesty of the state defending them, and with regard to the actions of all men and especially princes where there is no court of appeal, we must look at the final result (Musa, 1964). Such kind of situation is not prevalent in democracies because the leaders cannot afford to adopt such a thinking as they have always the fear of getting exposed by the opposition parties and vigilant press. However, in totalitarian systems, where the leaders have extraordinary control of the different variables can think of having such kind of attitude. In democracies, the policy makers have to be constantly vigilant so that the policies may not go against the accepted behaviour of the public.

When we talk of bargaining, competition, command, conflict and co-operation as the possible styles for policy decision making, it so seems that the policy making process as such includes the executive, legislature, administrative agencies, interest groups etc. and the whole of the process resolves around these institutions and actors. These agencies have been termed as proximate policy makers by Lindbloom. He says, except in small political system that can be run by something like New England town meeting, not all citizens can be immediate, or proximate, makers of policy. They yield the immediate or proximate task of decision to a small minority (Lindbloom, 1968). We normally take the role and activities of these proximate decision-makers as the complete policy making process and hence keep on concentrating on their roles only. Infact, the part played by the proximate policy-makers, definitely quite and important and significant, is at the final stage of the cumbersome policy-making process. As we get abundant information about the role being played by the important and immediate policy formulators, therefore, majority of us confine only with this part of the game and we completely forget the activities of the various non-governmental associations, institutions, and mass media in the process of policy decision making.

If the policy formulation process as a whole is viewed, the first thing comes as the policy problem or demand. Afterall, at this stage the proximate policy makers are not involved in making people to demand something from them in the shape of policies. Certainly, this will take place on the initiative of some persons, groups other than interest groups or associations. In case, the point gets raised here that the role of interest groups cannot be minimised in getting the problems identified as policy problems, the answer is that the interest groups take only those points which suit them whereas the other voluntary agencies and associations attempt to get the genuine problems of the masses identified as policy problems and such agencies have no specific personal interests like those of interest groups, involved there in. Interest groups are also one of the proximate policy makers. When the immediate or proximate policy makers start their activities, the policy issues have already been made, goals and objectives of the policy has been set up, and the press has already informed the people about the policy to come in near future. The role of the proximate policy makers is to get it formally formulated and to work out the means by which it would be properly implemented. It does not mean than the role of proximate policy makers in the process is of minimised importance. Their role, infact, is so significant that it cannot be matched by any body else, what it meant is that there are certain other agencies also which are involved, which work for the policies to be formulated, and which initiate in some cases for the identification of the policy issues, where from actually the process starts.

REFERENCES

1. The politics, political system and the policies cannot be separated from the environment and its forces.
2. Eulau, Heing and Prewitt, Kenneth, Labyrinths of Democracy : Adaptations, Linkages, Representation, and Policies in Urban Politics, Indianapolis, Bobbs-Merrill, 1973.
3. This statement is aptly applied in practical or real life.
4. Public Problems affects the men in one way or the other directly or indirectly.
5. Low, Theodore J., "American Business in Public Policy : Case Study and Political Theory," in World Politics, 1964.
6. It is true that we are living in a materialistic age. Men are more busy in his personal affairs.
7. Key, V.O., Public Opinion and American Democracy, New York, Knopf, 1967.
8. Public opinion changes as the winds change.
9. In every society, policy problems are identified and solved by the elites.
10. In framing of the public policy, government consults the elites.
11. Key, *op. cit.*
12. Barnard, C.I., The Functions of the Executive (Cambridge, Mass, Harvard University Press, 1964).
13. The conflict and consensus are the two important parts of politics.
14. Bass, B.M., Organisational Decision Making and Social Issues (Hinsdale, III, Richard D. Irwin, Inc., 1983).
15. The representatives of the people are the agents of the masses.
16. March, J.M. and H.A. Simon, Organisation (New York, John Wiley and Sons, Inc., 1958).

17. Simon, H.A., Administrative Behaviour (New York, The Free Press, 1947).
18. It is true that the executive is accountable and answerable to the legislature.
19. Naisbitt, J. Megatrends, Ten Directions Transforming Our Lives (New York, Warner Books, Inc. 1982).
20. The executive remains in power as long as it enjoys the support of the legislature.
21. Bureaucracy is the operational branch of the government.
22. Dye, Thomas R., Understanding Public Policy, Englewood Cliffs, Prentice Hall, 1975.
23. Dye, *Ibid., op. cit.*
24. Espstein, Edward Jay, News from Nowhere, New York, Random House 1973.
25. Lindbloom, Charles, E, The policy making process, Englewood Cliffs, Frentice Hall, 1968.

5

POLICY IMPLEMENTATION

After the policy formulation process gets over, the issue, demand and proposal comes to be known as public policy. Where the policy formulation ends, implementation begins or starts.[1] The implementation of policy is equally important as the policy formulation is. The stage which is followed by the policy decision making phase is as significant as the policy making is. Unless the policy made is adequately implemented in a positive form, the prime purpose of making policy would not be fulfilled. At the implementation stage, the goals and the objectives the policy is meant to attain may be misinterpreted or negated, if the implementors do not perform their role effectively and efficiently.

At the time of making evaluation of policy alternatives for deciding the 'one best' the policy formulators must keep the implementation of the policy as one of the criteria in their minds. So many instances are there when the implementors had not acted on the right lines and then to achieve something beneficial the policy had spoiled the events. The Congress (I) government in India under the Prime Ministership of Mrs. Indira Gandhi made the policy for controlling the excessive population growth. The implementors acted in a manner which not only defeated the purpose, but also made public against the party. Forced sterlisation during the period of internal emergency by the implementors amounted to the trounced defeat of the party at polls in 1977. Furthermore, the Janata government had to make the things clear in absolute terms that the government wants to check the population growth, but with the co-operation of the people and not in a compulsory manner as the Congress (I) government did earlier. During the implementation, the hopes and aspirations of programme's sponsors either begin to be realised or altered beyond recognition. Policy future is probably more common than programme success.

It is very rare that the policies formulated are self-executing and is executed by the mere statement. Often the policies require some action for execution and implementation. The implementation process has certain activities working within it, such as issue and enforcement of directives, funds disbursement, loans and grant sanction, gathering and passing of information, roles and duties assignment among the personnel engaged in implementing, etc. Most of the activity surrounding policy implementation takes place within administrative or bureaucratic agencies.[2] The implementation of policies is largely done by the bureaucrats as they have control over the resources and legal powers of the government and thus are passed on directives to implement policies from the three organs of the government, that is, executive, legislature and judiciary. Though it is commonly felt that the political executives, which are the elected representatives of the people is democracies, perform the major task of implementing the policies.

According to Henry Kissinger, former U.S. Secretary of State, the outsiders believe a presidential order is consistently followed. Nonsense. I have to spend considerable time seeing that it is carried out and in the spirit the president intended (Halperin, 1974). Of course, the ultimate and final responsibility of implementing policies in proper form is that of the political executive, but in actual practice, this work is carried out by the bureaucrats. They are heading the full fledged departments of the government and are in the pipeline right from the top down to the bottom levels. It simply cannot be expected to implement the policy at every kind by the political executive. Though the bureaucrats and the officials are supposed to carryout the policies on the lines told by the political executive, yet there are so many instances when the bureaucrats use their own discretion in implementing a policy decision. The administrative agencies have the responsibility to perform the tasks of the governments in implementing policies, and thus these agencies have a qualitative bearing on the citizens

There was a time when it was considered that the task of making policies is that of the legislature and executive, and the implementation of the policies made by the government is to be done by the Administration. There used to be a hard and fast dichotomy between politics and administration, that is, between policy formulation and its implementation. It was strongly felt that the policies are made by the legislature and implemented in the executive organ by the administration.[3] This view was further supported by the origin of doctrine of separation of powers clearly making categories of the functions to be performed by the legislature, executive, and judiciary. Politics was concerned with the formulation of the will of the state, it was concerned with value judgements, with determining what government should do or should not do, and it was to be handled by the political branches of the government, that is, the legislature and executive (Goodnow, 1900). The task of the administration was to put into effect what has been decided by the government in the shape of public policy.

There has been a great controversy between the relationship of policy and administration especially in democratic political systems which are based on the principle of popular sovereignty and mass citizen participation—were administration simply considered an extension or part of the basic policy making process, its compatibility with democracy might not be a matter of great controversy. Part of what gives rise to the issue is that administrative organisation is most often structured hierarchically, particularly, with orders flowing from the top-down. Such top-down arrangements seem to conflict inherently with democracy, particularly when democracy is viewed in terms of mass citizen participation.[4] A strong counter argument can be must that an efficient organisation is necessary to implement what the legislators (the representatives of people) have decided should be policy, just as there is little question that political and social movements could not succeed without the organisational apparatus they have developed and acquired (Wasby, 1972). The politics administration dichotomy is no longer accepted.[5] The administration now attempts to find out the best way of implementing a policy in comparison to carry it out as suggested by the policy formulators. The 'delegated legislation' has further strengthened the ties of relationship between politics and administration. The legislator's lack of time, lack of interest, improper information and expertise amount to the authority to take decisions of implementation to the administrative agencies. Most of the policies are not self executing. Therefore, the authority to implement those is being passed on the administrative agencies.

1. *The Legislature* : The administration and implementation of public policy is also made by the legislature. If the policy initiated in the legislature is enacted by the legislature in full details, it would leave little choice with the administrative agencies and bureaucrats for implementing it is their own way. It sounds, more logical in democratic political systems that the policies should be discussed and enacted in detailed manner by the duly elected representatives of the people. Supposing the policy on improving educational standards and making the education job-oriented is being made by the legislature, and the legislature after getting information from the government departments on the kind of courses, both technical and professional, includes it in the policy statement, then it would leave little choice to the administrative and executing agencies to implement it on their own discretion. But in actual practice, the work load of the legislatures has increased upto such an extent that they normally do not find enough time to deliberate upon the issues.

2. *The Courts* : The courts also implement some of the policies. This normally happens when the policy is not clearly worded or different interpretation of a policy could be taken up. In such like cases, the court gives its verdict and whatever is decided by the court is normally considered ultimate last and final, unless the legislature again legislates on that.

3. *Interest Groups* : Since the legislature through 'Delegated Legislation' leaves certain points to be filled in the broad framework of policy by the administrative agencies, therefore, when the interest groups face unsuccess at the time of policy making by the legislature exercise their influence over the administrative agencies for implementing those points in the manner which suits the interests of these groups.

The preceding paragraphs reveal that the legislature courts, and interest groups play some role in the implementation of policies, but basically the policy implementation is the task of bureaucrats and administrative agencies. It is said that the policy would not attain its proper goals unless it is implemented properly.[6]

Problems of Implementors

The implementors have the following problems in their way of implementing the policies. These are Communication Resources and implementors inclinations (Edwards, 1979).

1. *Communication* : If you will imagine a communication system, you will realise that there is a great deal of variability about what comes out. The input and output can, therefore, be described in terms of their variance. If it is a good communication system, however, there must be some systematic relation between what goes in and what comes out. That is to say, the output will depend upon the input, or will be correlated with the input. If we measure this correlation, then we can say how much of the output variance or difference is attributable to the input and how much is due to random fluctuations of noise introduced by the system during transmission. So, we see that the measure of transmitted information is simply a measure of the input-output correlation

(Miller, 1967). The foremost requirement for implementing the policies in an appropriate manner is the proper communication to the implementors about what is to be done. The purpose of the policy must be clearly communicated to the implementors and the directions issued to them, must be conveyed to them inconsistent, clear and accurate terms. Whatever the decision has been made, it has to be properly transmitted to all the lower levels so that it could be adequately implemented.

We have referred to earlier that the courts are also the implementing agencies and the verdict or judgement of the court about a particular point of a policy or of whole of the policy is supposed to be carried out by all in a system unless it is changed by the higher court in the land or by the legislature. Supposing policy 'A' was enacted and an appeal was made against it in the court. The court gave its verdict, which is supposed to be carried out by all in a given system. Where is the guarantee that all the implementors and the implementing agencies will read about the decision of the court or the versions of the court decision taken up by the press men is going to be strictly on the lines of the decision made by the court. Would it not mean that the lack of proper transmission to all stands in the way of uniform implementation of the policy ? We have noted above that there is input-output correlation on the basis of communication. Therefore, it is required that the policies should be transmitted to all levels of implementation in a highly fool-proof manner. Of course, the administrative agencies and executive organ of the government have a better system of transmission than the courts, still, as it is to pass through so many stages and anything going wrong at any stage would distort the basic policy goals attainment because of proper implementation owing to inadequate transmission.

Moreover, the implementation cannot be carried out properly if the policy directives are not clear.[7] It is expected of the policy makers to issue policy statements in absolute clear manner and these should not be vague at all. The bureaucracy and the administrative agencies involved in the implementation have an hierarchical order. May be that the top man knows little bit about the policy and how it has to be implemented. He has to pass on detailed instructions to the middleman and the middleman to the lower man who actually has to implement the policy. If even one out of the three involved in the process becomes little vague, it would affect the whole of the policy in a substantial degree.[8]

Another significant problem in regard to the implementation is that the implementors are not present at the time of policy making. They get information through secondary sources only which often amounts to vagueness. Another requirement of communication for proper implementation is consistency required in the policy statements. The clauses of the policy should not be overlapping and all the points mentioned therein have to be consistent. India made policies on the establishment and growth of multinationals in the country for providing job opportunities to the people and for increasing the productivity in the country for the overall development of the country. Simultaneously, the implementors were not issued proper directives as to the controlling of multinationals from safety points of view or the implementors did not worry much to ensure safety measures. As a result of these lapses, large number of people died in Bhopal in 1984 owing to leakage of Gas from union carbide factory and still large number suffered incurable diseases for whole of their lives. The polices should be consistent in its approach and alongwith this, it should not hamper other policies in force in the system. The interest groups often play a significant role in policy formulation. The activities of these groups are mostly responsible of one policy decision overlapping the other. Let us suppose that interest group 'A' with its influence has been able to get a policy 'X' formulated and interest group 'B' has been in position to have policy 'Y' enacted suiting its interests. Policy 'B' has some point which overlap certain clauses of policy 'A'. In such like situations, would the implementors not be in jeopardy whether to execute policy 'A' or policy 'B'. This amounts to the point that the legislature and other policy maker actors have to be consistent in their approach at the time of making policies.

2. *Resources* : The implementation plan was a good idea. Setting these ambient air quality standards was a good idea. But what happens as we go along depends on what sort of resources we get as we move into the implementation phase of the plan (Jones, 1975). The absolute properly transmitted, clear and consistent directives on particular policy cannot be thoroughly implemented if the implementors do not have financial resources with them for properly carrying out the policy. Undoubtedly, every new programme needs money for its compliance. Of course, the policy-makers make provisions for the money for carrying out the policy goals effectively. But simply making provisions does not sort out the purpose.[9] Do we think that simply the announcement by the university authorities that the financial revisions have been made for establishing a computer centre at the campus will solve the purpose ? No, it would not unless the funds are made available in actual terms for the computer centre. Till the implementors do not get proper resources the policies can never be executed and always the policy makers shall have to cut a sorry figure.

Staff

Another impediment in the way of adequate implementation of public policies is that of staff. Most of the policies are unable to be appropriately carried out because of deficient staff. Many elements combine to make good administration.[10] Leadership, organisation, finance, morale methods and procedure, but great than any of these is man power (White, 1955). Thoroughly planned out policies fail to attain the proper goals without well competent personnel to handle those. Inadequate staff strength amount to the unsuccess in policy implementation. The personnel at work should be dynamic with a clear and consistent information to be able to put to use for effective implementation of the policies. They must be made aware to apply the policy intent in a uniform manner without using their discretion in implementing that. In the hierarchical set up, the officials at the top must ensure that the subordinates to carryout the policies are sufficiently in number and do it in an effective manner. The personnel assigned the task of implementation of policies, must be thoroughly trained and should know their area of job in a well-to-do manner so that they could do proper justice to the programme they have been told to take up. People in jobs have to be technically and professionally trained in order to let them handle the job of implementing the technical clauses in a desired manner.

At the outset we asked ourselves the question—what is the object of training ? If the answer is to attain the greatest degree of efficiency, then the word efficiency seems to need some closer definition. In any large scale organisation, efficiency depends on two elements, firstly, the technical efficiency of the individuals to do the particular work allotted to him and secondly, the less tangible efficiency of the organisation as a corporate body derived from the collective spirit and outlook of the individuals of which the body is composed. Training must have regard to both the elements. Training should endeavour to produce a staff member whose precision and clarity in the transactions of business can be taken for granted. The staff must be attuned to the tasks which they will be called upon the perform in changing circumstances. Training must be directed not only to enabling an individual to perform his current work more efficiently, but also to fitting him for other duties and, where appropriate, developing his capacity for higher work and greater responsibilities (Report, 1944). Staffing problems are faced more acutely when the policies of new nature and type are to be implemented. Either there is not enough money with the government to engage adequate staff, or if the money is even available, then the persons having specialised knowledge are not available to carry out the policies properly.

Information

Other than proper staff strength with technical and professionalised training, the staff agencies also require proper information about what is to be done and how it is to be done. In the absence of it probably the most efficient and well-trained personnel would not be in a position to effectively carry out the policies enacted by the government. Supposing the policy is formulated to give relief in the shape of subsidies to the agriculturists, the staff is definitely requiring to know that on which criterion the subsidies have to be given and to what extent. Improper information would never permit the staff to perform their tasks appropriately.[11] When a central decision maker is responsible for evaluating all information and making all decisions, rather than for making basic policy choices alone, his effectiveness in a large and complex system is diminished by several factors.

First, he can read or hear and understand only a limited quantity of information. All large organisation leaders complain of the volume of relevant communications crossing their desks and of the impossibility of handling it all. It is inevitably necessary to decentralise at least to the extent of letting a presidential staff, or its equivalent dispose of much of the incoming material that seems irrelevant or unworthy of the chief functionary's time. There is also increasing technical complexity of much relevant information. The leader cannot be even though he may be expected to be, a genuine expert in all fields of military technology, cost accounting, political manoeuvres, monetary inflation, urban transportation, or medical care. At various the raw data from the environment must be put in a form that can be interpreted by the top elite.

Authority

In the absence of proper Authority with the implementors the policies cannot be thoroughly implemented. Authority is an influence derived from willing acceptance by masses of implementors directives and to expect compliance with them. Authority always operates on the road of values.[12] It influences directly. It is based on reason. In other words, it is an art of reasoning. Authority may be featured as influence based on legitimacy. Any legitimate power is called as authority. Implementors have authority over masses because masses regard implementors claims upon them as rightful and legitimate. The authority establishes the relationship between the rulers and the ruled, policy formulators and policy implementors.[13] The authority relationship is subjective, psychological and moral in nature, in comparison to forms of influence based on use of material resources or physical coercion. Authority is also voluntaristic in operation. A person complies voluntarily because it is the right or appropriate thing to do. In political system, authority means that people are willing to follow rules, accept results, and abide by the judgement of governing officials. Authority is an important resource to implementors, in includes the power to go to the court to seek enforcement of an anti-discrimination law, to issue subpoenas for tax records, to issue orders to other officials, to withdraw funds from projects that are not being conducted according to the law, and to provide administrative funds, staff loans and technical advice and assistance to lower-level governments to help them implement a policy decided by a superior jurisdiction. Each of these powers increases the arsenal of resources that implementors have at their disposal to ensure that policies are carried out as intended. Although federal officials lack effective authority over state and local officials this task of control is nothing compared to their lack of authority over private individuals groups, and businesses, upon whom, the successful implementation of policies often depends. The courts also depend on private individuals and groups to guide the actions of public officials in implementing judicial decisions. Through their possession of resources such as money, prestige, and the mass media, local elites can shape public opinion and effect the tone and atmosphere of a community. Courts also depend on private parties to submit new cases that enable the judiciary to follow up on their decisions (Edwards, 1979).

3. *Implementors Inclination* : For the proper implementation of policies much depends on the personality and inclinations of the implementors. It is not only enough to know what is to be done and, how it is to be done, but along with it the implementors must have forceful wish to execute a policy on proper lines. And if this will be missing, it would hamper the implementation upto considerable extent. The officials to carry out the policies must be so trained that they should feel it obligatory on their part to carry out the programme in a well-

desired manner. The officials are neither depended upon the policy makers, that is, the legislature, which formally enacts the policies nor are they answerable to them. In such a situation it would amount to the use of discretionary will of the implementors to implement the policy in one way or the other.[13] Some people, assigned the role of implementation, have positive approach towards the goals, whereas some are born with negative approach.[14] When the things have been totally left to the implementors, would the ones with negative inclinations not go much beyond the expected levels, whereas the positive approach officials will go above the expectations. The policy implementation neither requires going above nor below the levels, but to put it to use according to the required standards. An implementor not willing to carry out the policy will behave in a manner which will decidedly hamper the 'policy goals attainment'. It is possible he may just ignore few of the specifications made by the formulators or by the senior officials for implementation of the policy properly. He can also take much more time for implementing the policy because of the prime reason that he is not that much in favour of the policy. Of course, if these lapses on the parts of the implementors are pointed out, they can be put to questions and enquiries by the courts, higher officials, political executive, etc. But for bringing such things to the notice of top eachlon of officialdom, the masses need abundant and thorough awareness and knowledge, which is commonly lacking.

Implementation and Public-Positive Approach

The policies are formulated by the decision makers to be implemented in a given environmental structure. Mainly, the policies have influence and control over the society and its constitutions, that is, the human beings. The human beings behaviour has always remain a very complicated and complexed phenomenon to be understood by anybody in a highly clear manner.[15] The policies are meant to make people act according to the rules stated their-in, whether the reference is made to social welfare, education, industrial production, law and orders, agricultural growth, tax rates and subsidies, or better employment opportunity. Ultimately, it is the human beings on whom the policies are to be implemented and unless they extend their co-operation and willingly accept the policies the implementors cannot carry out these effectively and the goals the policy is supposed to attain will never be achieved. The policy formulators do keep in mind the environmental factors at the time of framing policies because they are in know of it that without the help of the masses the policies cannot be a success.[16]

We do not mean here that the attitude and behaviour of the masses is the utmost important criterion for the successful implementation of the policy, but simultaneously it is not that insignificant that we can afford to take the co-operation of the masses guaranteed on each and every policy. The issue of the acceptance of the policies by the masses has not been able to catch the attention of the social scientists mainly because of the view that the masses are always obedient to the rules framed by the government. But this is not the case suiting every occasion. If these are the things then why at all the crimes and other anti-society as well as anti-national acts would be committed, probably no government wants that the peace and amity should be disturbed within its jurisdiction or the crimes would take place. If we have to simply accept the legalistic approach to government then why people should not follow these policies of the government which are against the crime and anti-society acts. The study of policy process remains incomplete if we do not bring into the factors responsible for the public, positive support and negative approach towards the acceptance of policies enacted by the governmental institutions and actors. The major factors, depicting the positive approach of the public towards policies and the role of implementors to that effect are (Anderson, 1966).

1. The human beings are mainly of the view to abide by the introductions and directives of those who are, superior to them. In democracies, the people elect their representatives to take care of their interests and demands. The elected representatives are fully competent, according to the masses,

to frame governing rules for them. We have an inclination to obey the policies and rules framed by the government. In society, there are always a thin and slender majority of those who do no abide or care for the rules of the government. Right from the birth of a child, he is taught to obey and abide the parents and elders at home, teachers at educational institutions instructions at technical workshops, superiors at office and these behavioural characteristics rather compel the individuals not to disobey the policies of the government. In other words, the man gets used to obeying the authority of those whom he considers superior to him. The respect to authority and obedience to the government policies has relationship to the psychological and moral make-up of the individuals. No one wants to be termed as 'Law Breaker'.

2. When the people elect the governors or rulers they have it definitely somewhere in their minds that the elected ones would make rules which will benefit the masses. Supposing a policy on agricultural production and food grains prices has been made. The section of agriculturists will definitely obey the policy and help in every possible way would be extended by them to the implementors for its earlier and effective execution. Supposing another policy regarding industrial labourers, and third regarding employment opportunities have been made. Whereas the industrial labours and unemployed will like the policies to be carried out at the earliest they would also expect other sections of the society not being directly benefitted to comply with the policies and inturn the industrial labourers and unemployed persons would be complying with the policies suiting other sections of the society. Therefore, this give and take among the masses regarding obedience to the policies smoothens the way to the policies implementation.

3. Majority of the individuals view the policies in terms of logic and reasons. People normally do not have the habit to negate or disobey a point whom they feel is justified. Of course, here it becomes obligatory on the part of the implementors to attempt to convince people. A convinced lot will not disobey the policies even if these hamper them. People foot the bills

for the electricity consumed or other public utility services utilised by them. Whey should they not pay the amount and put the questions that when the government pays for its officials why the government does not pay for the consumers. But people do not question or challenge it and keep on doing it because they are convinced that as they have to pay the price for getting a service from a private organisation, similarly they have to pay to the government also.

4. Another reason for the public obedience to the policies enacted by the government is the rightful thinking of the masses and the government policies are legitimate and have been made by the appropriate authority by following a correct procedure. Legitimacy is the quality of being justified or willingly accepted by the subordinates, that is, the masses, that converts the exercise of political power, this is, policies into rightful authority. It reflects an underlying consensus that endows the governmental officials with authority, and that offers respect and acceptance for government institutions and its policies. We have discussed above that the courts also play their role in implementing the policies. A decision of the court is taken more seriously by the people in regard to a policy even in comparison to the decision made by the legislature on the policy.

5. The policies in accordance with the existing and well-established traditions and conventions are very easily accepted by the masses. Nobody wishes to raise his finger on a point which is going on well in the sphere. It is universally accepted that on Sundays all establishments, offices, and business centres would be closed, why the rules are like this that the railways, telecommunication, libraries etc. would not be closed on Sundays ? Why the people working in these departments do not disobey the policies ? Mainly, because of the factor that they know that these establishments are meant for providing effective services to the public and hence, these cannot be closed.

6. Majority of the persons in the society have the wish to be known as respectable persons in the society. They never

want to be termed as law breakers or anti-society and anti-national elements. This thinking rather compels the persons to abide by the government policies because they are in know of it that once they are pointed out as not acting in accordance to the policies of the government, they would have a stigma and slur on their names and personality, ultimately leading to loss of status and respect among the members of the society.

7. The policies have sanctions of law behind them and the violators are liable to be imprisoned, find or punished for their acts. These fears also make the public to not to act in a manner whereby they can be penalised by the government through its adjudicating agencies. A person who steals a bread for the first time must have thought over it so many time before doing it, whereas a professional thief will not mind doing it. The reason is that who has not done it earlier will be scared of the punishment so many times earlier because of which he is not bothered. The professional of this kind are comparatively much less than ordinary law-abiding and peaceful citizens who feel scared of breading the policy or obstructing in its implementation in any way.

8. We have referred to above that the public accepts and comply with the government policies because it is in habit to extend respect to the authority and legitimately enacted policies. This amounts to the deliberate, spontaneous, and voluntary will of the people to conform to the policies of the government. The force or coercive methods of punishment on penalising by the government cannot compel the masses much to offer their acceptance readily to the policies as their free will and genuine intentions can. Supposing all the people make it a point not to deposit the tax, does it mean that the government can use force and coercive methods on all. Therefore, the voluntary will of the people to abide by the policies helps the policies to be implemented properly and in an appropriate manner.

9. It is commonly felt that people have a short memory and they forget the things in an earlier span of time. In June 1984, when operation Blue Star took place in Punjab, people had

thought this issue will never be forgotten by the common masses. With the passage of time things have been settled down in a peaceful and cordial manner. As the time will keep on getting away, people would be getting more familiar to the policies and their motives and these would be slowly and gradually accepted by the public.

Implementation and Public-Negative Approach

All the policies enacted, framed or formulated by the government are not followed obeyed and complied by the masses in totally. If the people had shown all the obedient regards to the policies, probably more than half of the problems of the governments would have been over. The human beings have the tendency to posses both positive and negative thinking traits. It depends upon the circumstances and the individuals being affected or influenced by them. When people feel at large that the policy is fundamentally against their basic rights and privileges, they will try their best to defy these policies and would obstruct in the way of its being properly implemented. We had referred to morality as a basic factor for accepting the policies by the public. But there are no measuring sticks whereby one could say how much of morality is required and from which section of the society. Morality in itself is a subjective phenomenon and varies from individual to individual. If 'A' feels it is his moral obligation to respect his parents, it is not necessary 'B' will also think on the same lines. Moreover, human behaviour is quite dynamic and for away from being static. A person who has remained confined and attached to moral issues may turn up as an immoral on some count and still there would not be any parameters to convince him that he has become immoral on this particular count. The individuals have a natural instinct of defending their actions as right even if the others say that it is wrong.[17]

The major reasons for the public not accepting the policies are as such :

1. We have discussed in the preceding chapters the role of the interest groups in policy-making. Interest groups struggle to get such kinds of policies which suit their

self-ends. The interest groups can also apply a negative role in amassing the public opinion to not to obey a policy which basically harms the interests of the group. Moreover, the individuals who feel that with the policy they are going to loose considerably they would attempt their best to stand in the way of the implementation of the policy irrespective of the factor whether they have regular membership of an interest or pressure group or not. In such line situations persons being affected may join hands with each other and form an association or group to fight against the policy. The government of Punjab dismissed the adhoc lecturers in government colleges in Punjab in 1980. The dismissed lecturers formed an association and field a write petition in the Supreme Court to get relief. The court verdicted in their favour and the persons are continuing since 1979, whereas the case is still pending with the Supreme Court for final orders;

2. Proper communication including fool-proof transmission, clarity, and consistency is required for the policy to be thoroughly implemented. The masses should also be made to understand the policy and its goals and objectives at length so that they may develop the feeling to obey to same. The policies equivocal and ambiguous in terms and references would not be easily obeyed by the masses for the simple reason that they would not be in a position to understand the same. Lack of proper information to the public about the policies stands in the way of public's ready acceptance and obedience to the policies. The governmental institutions and implementors should try to educate the masses about the policies;

3. People weight the policies in terms of its values and force. According to Clinard, selective disobedience of law is closely related to the law-value conflict (Clinard, 1957). It is a natural human habit to comply with the aspect which seems more drastic. Supposing a person

comes across a snake and dog simultaneously, he will first of all try to save himself from snake in comparison to dog because he feels and thinks more danger from snake. Same is the case with the policies. People feel scared of getting severe punishment of being caught for committing criminal acts, therefore, they normally avoid doing these whereas they are not that much bothered about doing civil disobedience if suiting their interests. People view the policies in terms of punishment they can have for breaking those. It does not mean that the regulations have less or no punishments, if being broken by the public, are not at all accepted by the masses. Here we should not forget that the overall strength of law-breakers is much less in comparison to law-abiders;

4. Overlapping in various policies is also a factor for people's not obeying them. Because such like situations normally confuse the masses as to which policy is to be obeyed in which circumstances and which is not to be obeyed; and
5. The rules and policies which touch the religious and cultural sentiments of the public are not easily digested by the masses. The Army attack on the religious shrines of the Sikhs in Punjab in 1984 has not been taken by the community in good taste. We have analysed in the proceeding chapter that environmental factors are kept in view by the policy framers at the time of making policies. The governmental institutions normally try not to make any such policy which will hamper the religious, cultural, social and other environmental issues because they know such policies cannot get acceptance of the masses in general.

The policy-implementation is mainly the task of the bureaucrats and administrative agencies working at different rungs of administration within a system. The public gets in touch with the officials on almost every problems being faced by them. The officials should try to create good relations with the public so that they may agree to their views. Firstly, whenever a policy is to be implemented, the implementors should educate the masses about the objectives, motives and goals of the policy so that the people come to know about the same. The implementors should try to convince the masses that the policy is reasonable, logical and legitimate and has been made to the benefit of the society. The masses should be persuaded to obey the policies. If the people have respect for authority and legitimacy, it should not be exploited by the implementors through harassment of the masses on one count or the other. The officials should try to win the confidence of the people and they should not depict their discriminating attitude towards particular individuals at local levels or higher levels.

Secondly, the policy enacted should be widely and fairly propagated through all the means available with the government so that the masses are made to feel good about the policy. The policy should be overall in the interests of the society and the people should be made aware of it so that they may feel like having the policy. Thirdly, the implementors should make minute survey before implementing the policy and the area or section of people, they feel, will stand in the way of proper implementation should be taken proper care of at the actual implementation stage so that the things do not distort further and those who are against the policy should be persuaded to agree by that. Fourthly, the benefits which the people are to get because of the policy should be immediately passed on to them. This would further smoothen the way of the policy being implemented because when the people would get benefits they would not mind paying also for certain provisions made in the policy, so this give and take should be in process and a proper balance should be made by the implementors between plus and minus points of the policy (of course, minus from the consideration of public only). Fifthly, the interests of the particular communities being protected by the policy should be thoroughly highlighted by the implementors for getting a section of people with them and to fight the struggle to be made, if at all, by the other sections of the society. It is again, more or less, in the nature of the human beings to come forward and join hands with each other where they are to get some benefit individually or collectively. Sixthly, where all these factors stated above fail to get proper response from the public, the implementors should not feel reluctant to use force and other methods of the sort. After all, the policies have the sanction of law behind them and the government officials are empowered and duty bound to implement those. But it should be the last method only.

Conscious human behaivour involves making choices among alternatives deciding to do somethings and not to do others. There are essentially three ways in which administrative agencies, or other governmental bodies, concerned with implementing public policy can influence people to act in the desired ways—to select behavioural alternatives that result in policy compliance. First, to achieve a desired result agencies can strive to shape, alter or utilise the values people employ in making choices. Educational and persuasional activities are illustrative of this type of activity. Second agencies can seek to limit the acceptable choices available to people as by attaching penalties to undesired alternatives and rewards or benefits to desired alternatives. Third, agencies can try to interpret and administer policies in ways designed to facilitate compliance with their requirements. More than one of these alternatives are normally used in seeking compliance with a given policy (Anderson, 1979).

Policy making process is not complete only with the taking up of the decision on a particular issue making it as a policy. The policy implementation is equally important as the policy decision making is.[18] It can have almost an equal amount of impact on the issue as the decision making itself has on the issue. The policies formulated are not implemented in an automatic manner, but the governmental institutions, officials, administrative agencies, and even the non-governmental actors and associations play a considerable role both individually and collectively, for implementing the policies properly. The bureaucrats, the legislature, the courts the interest groups all possess a significant place in the implementation process. The government has to ensure proper communication, including transmission, clarity, and consistency in the policy directives, alongwith providing adequate resources, both material and staff, for proper implementation of the policies. The positive and negative approach of the public towards the obedience, compliance, disobedience, and non-compliance of the policies also has its place in the implementation process. The steps stated above are neither easy to be adopted without qualitative efforts, nor the policy makers, having sensitivity to the implementation problems, can afford to do away with any one of these.

REFERENCES

1. This is an idea taken from the book entitled 'Public Administration', written by Vishnoo Bhagwan and Vidya Bhushan.
2. Pressman, Jeffrey L.; Wildavsky, Aron B., Implementation, Berkeley, University of California Press, 1973.
3. Halperin, Morton H., Bureaucratic Politics and Foreign Policy, Washington, Brookings Institution, 1974.
4. Goodnow, Frank J., Politics and Administration, New York, Russel and Russel 1900.
5. Wasby, Stephan L., Political Science—The Discipline and Its Dimensions, Calcutta, Scientific Book Agency, 1972.
6. Edwards, George C., Sharkansky, Ira, The Policy Predicament, New Delhi, Allied Publishers, 1979.
7. Edward George, *op cit*.
8. Moynihan, Daniel P., Maximum Feasible Misunderstanding, New York, Free Press, 1969.
9. Jones, Charles O., Clean Air, The Policies and Politics of Pollution Control Pittsburgh, University of Pittsburgh Press, 1975.
10. White, L.D., Introduction to the Study of Public Administration, New York, Macmillan, 1955.
11. Almond Gabriel A. and Powell, G.B., Comparative Politics : A Developmental Approach, New Delhi, Amerind Publishing Co., 1975.

12. Edwards, George C. Sharkansky, Ira, *op. cit.*
13. Anderson James E., "Public Economic Policy and the Problem of Compliance : Notes for Research," Houston Law Review IV, 1966.
14. Anderson, James E., Public Policy-Making, New York, Holt, Rinehart and Winston, 1979.
15. Clinard, Marshall B., Sociology of Deviant Behaviour, New York, Holt, Rinehart and Winston, 1957.
16. Anderson, James E., *op. cit.*
17. Edwards, George C. Sharkansky, *op. cit.*

6

POLICY EVALUATION

The policy making process is quite a lengthy and detailed one. It not only deals with the identification of the policy issues and problems for making policies on those, but also to effectively and efficiently implement or enforce or execute or carry out those and to measure its outcome and impact on the society. Policy evaluation is practically as old as the policy and since the very beginning, the policy framers have been attempting to know the impact of the policies made by them through the policy evaluation. Policies are goal oriented and aim at the improvement of society for making it worth living.[1] The policy evaluation means policy assessment. The policy evaluation plays its role not only after the formulation and implementation of the policy but it starts right from the identification of various issues for making policies and putting those on policy agenda after viewing the various alternatives from various angles and selecting the 'one best' required according to the need of the time. The prime purpose of the evaluation is to measure the impact of the policies and the goods delivered to various sections of the society with the actual implementation of the policy. We had discussed earlier the input-output process for making policies. The output mainly tells us about rule-making, rule-application, and rule adjudication, whereas through evaluation we aim to know the outcomes of the output.

The policy evaluation is made in accordance to the

ideology, personal interests, party affiliations and other such like factors. Supposing 'A' evaluates the policy in the capacity of the political executive, he is liable to bring all the good points of the policy, whereas when 'B' belonging to the opposition will evaluate the same policy, he would bring to note all the points which go against the policy. Evaluation, of its own, is such a process which has element of subjectivity involved in it. People make the evaluation in accordance to the parameters of their own thinking and interests. A policy giving tax rebate to the people will be evaluated by the party in power as quite good because so many people got relief because of it.[2] The basic point may be that such a policy increases the number of votes to be polled by the party in the next elections. The opposition parties will evaluate the same policy from different perspectives. Such a kind of policy evaluation is not fair because there is no standard method involved in it to measure the actual impact of the policy, rather it has been measured depending on the evaluators personal ends.

The policy evaluation is also made on the basis of the actual working of the policy. The queries normally put forth to evaluate the policy are—whether the policy has been put to use in an efficient, effective and fair manner? How much the policy has cost the exchequer? Who are the beneficiaries and who have suffered losses and upto which extent? What is the role of implementors, are they earnestly executing it? Have the proper procedure been followed in implementing the policies? What are the views of the public about it, are they happy or sour about the policy? Such kind of evaluation can be made only through best of the efforts being made by the evaluators because it needs proper data collection and analysis beforing reaching to the conclusion about the fair or unfairness of the policy *vis-a-vis* societal goals and requirements. This type of evaluation has further led to the 'systematic' evaluation of the policies, which is quite common these days.

The protagonists of systematic evaluation are of the view that when the evaluation is to be made, it must be thoroughly objective and systematic. The evaluators mean to know the impact and outcome of the policies, on the basis of which they have to modify, amend or alter the policies. The systematic evaluation is made by keeping before the detailed information about the policy. Supposing policy 'A' is to be evaluated. The systematic evaluator would like to know where from the demand for policy 'A' came, who supported it, which other alternative demands and issues the policy framers had analysed and considered before making selection of issue 'A' far being on agenda and making draft legislation on policy proposal 'A', what are the prime objectives and goals of the policy, how any people and from which sections of the society are going to gain directly and indirectly with the policy A? Such type of points are especially taken note of by the systematic evaluators of the policy before going in for answers to the questions, whether the policy has attained or is attaining its goals and objectives? Whether the persons who actually demanded for such a policy have gained because of it on not? How many people are getting benefits in an indirect manner? Had the policy not been made what would have been the consequences? etc.

On the basis of systematic evaluation, the policy makers and the general masses come to know about the outcome of the policy. The biggest of the evaluation is that the government can modify, repeal, or amend any clause of the policy, if it is not suiting its objectives in totality and moreover, by knowing the impact of policy through evaluation and moreover by knowing the impact of policy through evaluation, the public will not hesitate in extending its full cooperation to the implementors of that policy in case of any difficulty or problem arising at implementation stage. Sometimes, evaluation is also made for not all that praiseworthy and commendable reasons. Programme decision makers may turn to evaluation to delay a decision, to justify and legitimate a decision already made, to extricate themselves from controversy about future decisions by passing the buck, the vindicate the programme in the eyes of its constituents, its finders, or the public to satisfy conditions of a government or foundation grant through the ritual of evaluation (Weiss, 1972).

Policy evaluation is also made on cost-benefit relationship, drawn mainly from the economies. It can be understood like this :

$$K \times 10 - KC\,3 = KA\,7$$
$$MY\,10 - MC\,12 = MA - 2$$

In this equation K and M are the two policy alternatives and *x* and *y* are the benefits, with C as the cost. In the first alternative benefits are more than the cost, whereas in the second the cost exceeds the benefits. Obviously policy K would be preferred and rated better in such like evaluation than policy M. Such an evaluation is made in the terms of gains being delivered to the masses and the losses suffered and have definitely to be evaluated in the terms of goals attained by those. It is true that no policy could be such which would provide benefits to all the persons in the society. If taxes are recovered for the benefit of the smooth provision of things to all then it certainly displeases the tax payers. The policy is evaluated in the proportion of positive and negative factors to different sections of the society, and of a policy comes to the rescue of 70% of the population and 30% are the loosers then definitely the policy is evaluated as beneficial. There are certain problems for policy evaluation on cost benefit calculations. The problem with cost benefit calculations is that psychological considerations too easily enter our specifications of costs and benefits, once they have entered, measuring such factors on an objective scale providing comparisons among activities is extremely difficult (Frohock, 1979).

Though, the policy evaluation is quite significant and does help to know the prime impact and attainments of the policies, on the basis of which the governments chalkout their further programme of action, yet not much attention is paid to it by the government and it so seems that neither the government has the time, nor the wish to make evolution of policies. A sincere and ingenuous report on federal evaluation in U.S.A. says, the most impressive finding about the evaluation of social programmes in the federal government is that substantial work in this field has been almost non existent. Few significant studies have been undertaken. Most of these carried out have been poorly conceived. Many small studies around the country have been carried out with such lack of uniformity of design and objective that the results rarely are comparable or responsive to the question facing policy makers. There is nothing akin tc a comprehensive federal evaluation system. Even within agencies orderly and integrated evaluation operations have not been established. Finding has been low. Staffing has been worse, forcing undue reliance on outside contractors by agencies that lack the in-house capacity to monitor contract work. The most clear-cut evidence of the primitive state of federal self-evaluation lies in the wide spread failure of agencies even to spell out, programme objectives. Unless goals are precisely stated, there is no standard against which to measure whether the direction of a programme or its rate of progress is satisfactory (Wholey, 1970).

Impact of Public Policy

The value, significance, and result of public policy is known through policy evaluation. In the words of wholey, policy evaluation is the assessment of the overall effectiveness of a national programme in meeting its objectives, or assessment of the relative effectiveness of two or more programmes in meeting common objectives (Wholey, 1970). Binner held the view that we should reserve the name 'programme evaluation' for when we are referring to a comprehensive evaluation of the entire system under consideration, and all it 'Problem or Procedural Evaluation' when we refer to some segment within the system (Binner, 1976). Policy evaluation research is the objective, systematic, empirical examination of the effects ongoing policies and public programmes have on their targets in terms of goals they are meant to achieve (Nichmias 1979), Wholey and Nichmias opinion about policy evaluation is to view policy from the goals and objectives attained by the policies. It is not that easy to be aware of the goals or objectives of the policies as they can be indirect also at times than being direct and clear in all the policies. Therefore, it goes in the fitness of the things to provide attention to the overall consequences of the policies through knowing the impact of the public policy.

We have referred to the distinction between policy outputs and outcomes. For knowing the impact and evaluation it is quite required to be aware of the policy outputs and then to measure in terms of outcomes or impact on society. The activities of the government with regard to increasing literacy levels in the country, better roads, well equipped health centres in rural areas, etc. can be termed as some of the outputs of various policies. Their outcome can be measured by knowing how many people per one thousand have attained the minimum literacy levels in comparison to the parts, whether the roads are in proper shape now, and how many people come to the urban areas now from the rural areas having treatment of minor and common diseases. The impact of the policy can be measured by seeing the change the system had undergone with the execution of the policies. Policy evaluation aims at knowing the policy impact in reality.[3] What are the objectives of the policy? By which programmes those have to be accomplished? And, what has been really achieved? Are some of the questions required for evaluating the policies. For knowing the impact, we also have to be sure to determine whether the change has taken place because of the policy or because of certain other factors. For example, to say that few people come to city hospitals now because of the policy to well-equip the hospitals in rural areas. We have to be sure whether it is because of the better facilities being made available in the rural hospital or because of the factor that in city hospitals nobody cares for the ruralities.

For proper evaluation of the policies, the following dimensions of the impact of policy have to be taken into consideration (Dye, 1981).

1. *Impact on the Target Situation or Group* : It can be known only if first of all the situation and group who is to be benefitted is very clearly defined. It must be made clear—who is to get the benefits and in what terms. Followed by it should be the determining of the desired effect of the programme. For

example to know whether the change would be in terms of relief in tax or more subsidies to increase the production. In case, the effects are combined, means the relief in tax as well as more subsidies for increased production, and both have to be given, then the things would be complexed and complicated because in such like situations, the priorities have to be fixed and the programme is to follow accordingly.

2. *Impact on Situations or Groups Other Than the Target* : Of course, it is very different to say that a policy has a policy has effect on particular group or situation. All policies more or less, have discriminatory, effects on various sections of the society. Let us suppose a policy pertaining to opening more avenues has been made for the unemployed graduates. Would it not mean that other than helping the unemployed youth, it has been able to increase the monthly income of the family whereby their economic prosperity has increased and the family has got more purchasing power leading to a better status of life and meaning better education for the dependent children in the family. It is rarely seldom that a policy has impact on a particular group and situation. Therefore, the policy evaluation should be made by taking into account the impact of other situations and groups than the target.

3. *Impact on Future as well as Immediate Conditions* : Policies may have impact on present conditions as well as on future conditions. It will depend whether the policies are of a short-range to deal with a present problem or demand, or it is aimed at to achieve gains in a longer span of time. Of course, the policies made for short term objectives if get abundant success can be translated into long-term programmes. The impact of the policies also has to be measured on the basis of the period the policy is meant to cover. However, there can be some policies which will serve both the purposes that is, to solve the present problem, and to be useful in the times to come also. For example, a policy made to curb the anti-national activities in a particular area can be successful in controlling these activities presently and can also be of success to have check on such kinds of activities in future. The impact in such like

cases shall have to be measured taking both the activities and their control by the policy in consideration.

4. *Direct Costs Terms of Resources Devoted to the Programme* : It is another dimension for evaluating the policy. We have discussed earlier also, the cost-benefit calculations to know the amount of money spent or being spent on a programme and its proportion to the total expenditure of the government. It is also reveals the amount of importance given to the programme *vis-a-vis* other programmes of the government. Let us suppose that during 1990 a government had the following programme areas and the funds were accorded in this proportion. Defence 20%, Agriculture 15%, Industry 15%, Education 10%, Health Programme 10%, Housing, Roads, Sanitation, Water 15%, Rural Development 15%. If during 2000's the government increased the agriculture programmes and spent 15% on it in comparison to 15% during 1990s and the amount was taken from industrial programmes, it means the government has attached more significance to agriculture than industry. The evaluation could be made on the basis why government neglected industry? What change the more of agricultural programmes did bring in? How much agriculture production was increased and how did it help the overall needs of the system? etc.

5. *Indirect Costs, Including Loss of Opportunities to do Other Things* : This is the fifth dimension for evaluating the policy. It is certainly not easy to be aware of the indirect costs of policy programmes. Since indirect costs are not quantified, therefore, it is very rarely included in formal decision making. It is rather impossible to measure the costs of inconvenience, dislocation, and social disruption caused by a slum-clearance programme. What are the indirect symbolic costs for the Hindus of the governments activities on behalf of the Muslims? As it is difficult to determine indirect costs, similarly it is difficult to measure indirect benefits of policies for the society. The policy regarding more job avenues for the weaker sections will amount to their better standards of life and more education and awareness in the family. It is difficult to measure these benefits and awards quantitatively.

6. *Policy Impact Includes Both the Symbolic and Tangible Effects of the Policy* : It is the ultimate, last and final dimension for evaluating the policy. Symbolic outputs include affirmation of values by elites, displays of flags, troops, and military ceremony, visits by royalty or high officials, and statements of policy or intent by political leaders and are highly dependent on tapping popular beliefs, attitudes and aspirations for their effectiveness (Almond, 1975). The society does not undergo real changes because of the symbolic outputs. No one will learn how to respect our nation simply by hearing a speech of a national leader unless the person is convinced that the national leader has a national character. People would not that much object the government failure in getting them better means to live as much as the fingers would be raised if the government will not try to do anything to that effect. Individuals, groups and whole societies frequently judge public policy interms of its good intensions rather than its tangible accomplishments. The general popularity and public appraisal of a programme may be unrelated to the real impact of a programme interms of desired results. The implication is that very popular programmes may have little positive impact, and *vice-versa*.

The policies of government may tell us more about the aspirations of society and its leadership than about actual conditions, they also help hold men together and maintain an orderly state. There was a time when politics was described as 'who gets what, when, and how.'[41] Now, it seems that politics centres about 'Who feels what, when, and how.' Systematic policy analysis concentrates on what governments do, why they do it and what difference it makes. It devotes less attention to what governments say. Perhaps, this is the weakness in policy analysis. Our focus has been primarily upon activities of governments rather than the rhetoric of governments (Dye, 1981).

. It is in most of the cases that the evaluation of the impact of policy is made by the government itself. The political executive as well as the legislature, the two major actors in the policy enactment, feel concerned to know about the changes the policy could bring about in the society and the real benefits or losses people have got because of it.[5]

The members of the political executive as well as legislators themselves also try to know about the policy from the people they meet. More often, this work is assigned to various government departments to present to the executive their findings derived through talks, hearings, discussions, both in formal and informal manner, with the people in writing in the shape of some reports. Another measure adopted by the government to determine the impact is the various teams of the legislators, bureaucrats, and other administrative agencies to personally visit the areas and sections of society to know from there the virtual impact of the policies on the people and the extent to which the goals of the policy have been attained and objectives accomplished. Moreover, the various government departments have it obligatory on their part to report to the political executive about the work done by their departments in regard to the policies. Supposing a policy on reducing the umemployment has been enacted. It would be the duty of the department to report how many unemployed persons were there before the execution of the new policy and what has been the net outcome of the policy now in reducing the number of unemployed. Such kind of data collected by the departments make the picture somewhat clear to the policy formulators.

The mass media plays a significant role in depicting the overall impact of the policy and the changes induced by it in the society[6]. The press, especially, has an important place in such kind of situations because the press correspondents give the news on the basis of primary information collected by them and for such an important news or feature challenging or speaking in favour of a policy they normally do not depend upon secondary source of information for the simple reason that the prestige and repute of the paper would be drastically effected if their news prove false or baseless. Furthermore, the government can also know about the impact of the policy on the basis of the complaints to that effect lodged by the public.

Let us suppose that the government propagated that all the persons belonging to weaker sections of the society will be entitled for the benefits of reservation for seeking admission, getting job, and for certain other such like measures. The complaints made by the members of the weaker section will reveal that the policy has not been able to have its positive impact on the society. Undoubtedly, it is again not a very sound method of determining the impact because most of the people either might not be knowing about the policy, or they might not be interested to file a complaint. Absence of any complaint should not be construed by the government that the programme is exceptionally well and has positive impact on society.[7]

There have been certain studies suggesting what measures can be adopted by the governments to be aware of the policies impact (Hatry, *et al.*, 1873). The appropriate evaluation of the policy can be made by comparing different situations. The evaluation means to know what has happened with a specific policy programme. Of course, this is always subjective and depends upon how one views the things. Most of the evaluation of policies comes to an end by knowing what the policy has made to happen in the society. Supposing a policy has been made to gear up the rural development. The government can satisfy itself that the programmes put to use become of the policy have amounted to the rural development. But more better it would be if the programme is also evaluated on the lines that if the policy had not been carried out what would have been its affect. The evaluators should try to compare two situations and from this the policy impact can be known more clearly.

The impact of the policies can also be determined by making comparison of those who are directly involved in a policy and those who are not.[8] Let us illustrate it by supposing that the government has made a policy on introducing 10 + 2 education system with the provision that during the +2 period the student will be imported vocational training and education for preparing the candidates for going to jobs after that. The impact can be measured by seeing that how many could get jobs after +2 in comparison to these who were not in 10+2 education system. The government gives on option to its employees of particular departments to go for an extensive training for two years. A and B are two groups. A group goes in for training whereas group B does not think it proper to undergo the training and term it as a futile effort. The comparison can be made between the two groups after sometime to know what the people from group A learned during training and how are they better than people belonging to group B.

For determining the impact of policy, the experimental situation is taken wherein are two groups one is control group and another is experimental group. Control group is the one which is not subjected to experimental treatment, whereas the experimental group is subjected to that treatment and then is compared with the control group in order to now the effects and impact of the stimuli provided to the experimental group. Of course, members of the control group are usually selected because of their presumed similarity to the members of the experimental group. Of course, from the research point of view, this experimentation seems to be quite fruitful and positive, but it is very difficult to demarcate the society into two groups because for doing so absolute control over the research universe is required and it goes beyond the control of the research cells to be able to manipulate the situation and exercise control over vast number of people being divided into two equal groups having close similarity to each other.

Policy Evaluation Four Concepts

Frohock has given the following four concepts Equity, Efficiency, Pareto Optimality and Public Interest, are helpful in evaluating public policy.

1. *Equity* : Equity means giving to each man his due, impartiality, uprightness, a system of supplementary law founded upon precedents and established principles. Equity is a branch of law that provides a remedy where the common law

does not apply. The common law is concerned largely with granting of damages after a wrongful action. It is designed to provide justice where damages may come to late to be meaningful. In an equity case, the court may order that something be done or forbid certain actions. Primarily equity means uprightness and fairness.[8] Though the policy formulators have been claiming since the beginning that the policies enacted by them are of fair and upright nature and kind meaning thereby that they believe in uplifting the standards in the society by adopting the measures whereby the needy and deserving could gain because of the policies formulated. Of course, it can be added here that the persons born on earth have right to share the things equally with all others of his type. In the democracies, the systems have provided the right to equality to all the persons irrespective of caste, creed, sex, and affluence. But what about the economic differences between the individuals. Why so much vast and glaring differences are between the individuals on account of wealth, money, property and life requirements. Should the policy formulators believe that inequality is the law of nature? No, they did not think so and try to make policies suiting the weaker and poorer sections of the society. How much these policies are able to serve the affected sections is of course a debatable question. We are mainly concerned here about the policy evaluation. First of all, the governments should bring about fair measures to evaluate policies and secondly, the policies enacted by the governments should be equitable because then only the policies can have desired and required impact on the society. The concept of equity can be helpful in evaluating public policies enacted by the government.

2. *Efficiency* : The determining of an action to be efficient or not is depended upon number of factors. The foremost important one is the disposition of the evaluator. How do you look at a particular action? What priorities you have in your mind? How fairly or poorly the action is rated by you? Are some of the questions which make the concept of efficiency as a subjective one. The normal and common human nature

speaks of getting subjective on the lines where the human beings are affected in one way or the other. However, it does not mean that the human beings are never objective so far as the opinion on concept of efficiency is concerned. Developing our point on this positive assumption of the human nature pertaining to the efficiency concept, it can be said that the policy evaluation can be made effectively by putting these queries : Have the goals of the policy been rightfully fixed? Are the goals in accordance to the demands of the people? Is the policy able to accomplish the goals it was supposed to do? Of course, the policy evaluators themselves have to behave very efficiently for being able to determine the impact of the policy. They have to clearly know the demands, the goals, and the effects in order to bring about the policy impact.[9]

3. *Pareto Optimality* : It is an evaluative criterion that states this—a social system is optimal if no person can be made better off without making at least one person worse off. Thus, a policy that makes one or several persons better off without hurting any one else is desirable under this criterion. A policy that helps some at the expense of others is accordingly undesirable. Two features of Pareto optimality make the criterion appealing. First, it resolves, by ignoring, the problem of interpersonal comparisons of value. We do not, with the Pareto criterion, have to judge whether one person is better or worse off than others, but only whether the person is better or worse off than previously. Second, it provides, infact, exclusively advertises, improvements that do not require losses. What could be more attractive to policy authorities than a social gain without a social loss? Some policies do not fair well under Pareto Optimality, for example, the welfare policy. Welfare is, in effence, social transfers, some are made better through the distribution of social resources, and distribution requires making some poorer by taking their wealth to make others better off. Does this mean that welfare always by definition fails to Pareto optimal test?

Let us look at welfare from a broader, and more controversial perspective. Some have maintained that the real purpose of welfare is to reduce civil disorder (Piven and Cloward, 1971). It is argued, for example, that giving relief is designed primarily to serve that larger economic and political order by insuring social stability and only secondary to give relief to the recipients. Supporting this argument is the fact that welfare policies are typically installed during periods of social disorders. Optimality means the wealthy gain by preserving social stability, the poor gain by getting assistance. Each class also loses, of course. The wealthy lose money, the poor are fixed more firmly in the system of prevailing inequalities. But are could also maintain that each class receives a net gain, thus remaining true to optimality.

4. *Public Interest* : The public is interested in law, not in the laws, in the method of law not in the substance, in the sanctity of contract, not in particular contract, in understanding based on custom, not in this custom or that. It is concerned in these things to the end that men in their active affairs shall find a 'modus vivendi', its interest is in the workable rule which will define and predict the behaviour of men so that they can make their adjustments (Lippman). The public is interested oftenly in the process through which the public policies are enacted. The major task and the responsibility of the government is to make policies which save the public interest. Of course, it is not that easy to distinguish between public and private interest. It sometimes so happens that people support a phenomenon or issue for the sake of others and they themselves have no direct interest involved in it. However, in an easy understandable manner one can say that the interest of the majority is the public interest.

Still it is rather difficult to define the concept of public interest in a well-formulated definition. If we view the public interest on the basis of majority strength, it even then does not bring out the clear sense. Because in majority it is often the minority in overall situation and sum total which has the victorious stand. Let us suppose that views of people on three different issues A, B and C are 45%, 30% and 25% respectively of the total population. It means 45% people have interest in issue 'A' and as it has more strength than for issues B and C, therefore, it is to be accepted. But why not to analyse it from other angle that 55% of the people are against issue A. It has been, that is why contended that whatever emerges out of the political struggle is public interest.

Redford has suggested three approaches for determining the nature of public interest (Redford 1958). Firstly, to view the areas of policies where there is much struggle among interest groups. It is also possible that various interest groups bargain and coordinate with each other for reaching to an accord for presenting an agreed public interest. Secondly, on attempt to highlight well accepted and continuously shared interests. These shared interests can be known as public interests. Thirdly, the necessity for organising and accepting procedure for the representation and balancing of interests for resolving issues, effecting compromise in policy enactment, and for executing policy properly.

The policies made by the government should be in accordance to the public interests.[10] At the time of determining the policy issues and demands, the decision making must take into account what the public policy actually wants and to what extent. The government should try to meet the challenges faced by the public through policies. After the policies have been implemented, the policy formulators and implementors should attempt to know the public interests being served through the policy put in use.

Policy Evaluation Problems

The policy evaluation is of course, a very significant phase in the overall policy formulation process. Policy evaluation, in most of the cases is being undertaken by the government through its various agencies, cells, and departments. However, the governments seldom attempt to get the policies evaluated through various sophisticated research techniques being used by various Research Institutes.[11] Through policy evaluation the cause and effect relationship can be known and on the basis of it certain modifications if required, can be made in the policy for its effective operation. It is certainly not easy to be aware of the exact impact of the policy. The problems which arise in the policy evaluation are as such :

1. The policy formulators should very clearly define the goals the policy is supposed to attain. Unless and until it is evidently depicted, it is very difficult to measure the impact of the policy. Not only the goals should be clearly stated, but these should also be properly communicated to the evaluators so that by keeping measuring criteria in view, the impact could be evaluated.
2. The policy evaluation task is normally performed by the government departments and agencies. The evaluators do not feel it safe to recommend to the politically superiors that the policy is unable to meet the requirements. The government should give free hand to the evaluators so that they may submit true picture.
3. The interests of the government has in sound propagation of the policies made by it. Especially in democracies, the party in power tries to have tailor-made reports about the positive policy impact so that it could justify its performance.
4. The untoward happenings and changes also stand in the way of appropriate evaluation of the policy. The policy is not made for the changes which took place after the enactment of the policy, therefore, it becomes difficult to measure the impact of the policy. The increasing population is a concrete example to it. Let us say that the public works department, as per the policy of the government, construct the roads. With the population increase, the traffic also increases and the roads constructed by the P.W.D. are not in a position to cope with the increase.
5. The heavy and huge financial and organisational investments made by the government in formulating and implementing the policies compel the evaluators not to find faults and defects in the policies.

6. The systematic evaluation of policy, huge amount of funds and time are required to be put to use in a conscientious manner. Different research techniques end to be used by a specially trained and qualified personnel recruited specifically for this purpose. Lack of it stands in the way of through policy evaluation.
7. The policy impacts are not specifically for a target group or section of society. The wide spread impacts of policies obstruct in the policy evaluation way. The policy affects favourably the other sections of the society also for which it was not directly made. An industry will not only increase production but also will give employment to various people whose standard of living will become better because of the employment and will also increase the purchasing capacity. Therefore, the policies with diffused impacts cannot be easily evaluated. As the gains cannot be evaluated, similarly, the losses cannot be measured in a tentative manner.
8. Systematic Data and information are required for evaluating the policy impacts. The difficulties in collecting data is one of the biggest problem in making evaluation of the policy. There would be so many persons in the society who would not like to be included in the list of informants. Such a kind of situation would be everywhere and the evaluators will feel the difficulty in gathering information about the policy from the public. In the absence of data, no evaluation of impact can be made.
9. Another problem in policy evaluation is the forcefulness and effectiveness of the evaluation report. Supposing an agency after evaluating a programme submits its report and it is negative. There are good amount of chances that the report would not be cared much about. But serious allegations and charges would be levelled against the evaluators. Because of such like cold, uncompromising and unhealthy attitude the evaluation reports are seldom negative.[12]

Two general laws to cover research on policy impact have been formulated (Wilson, 1973).

1. All policy interventions in Social problems produce the intended effect—if the research is carried out by those implementing the policy of their friends.
2. No policy interventions in social problems produced the intended effect if the research is carried out by independent third parties especially those skeptical of the policy.

Studies that conform to the first law will accept an agencies own data about what it is doing and with what effect, adopt a time frame (Longer/Short) that maximizes the probability of observing the desired effect, and minimise the search for other variables that might account for the effect observed. Studies that conform to the second law will gather data independently of the agency, adopt a short time frame that either minimises the chance for the desired effect to appear or, if it does not appear permits one to argue that the results are temporary "and probably due to the operation of the "Hawthorne Effect" (that is, the reaction of the subjects to the fact that they are part of an experiment), and maximise the search for other variables that might explain the effect observed (Wilson, 1973).

Public Policy Limitations

The analysis made in the present study reveals that the governments actions are depicted through the various policies enacted and implemented by it. With the assistance of the policies, a government can undertake any issue within the system. Of course, it has to be within the broad framework of the system's environment. Depending upon the needs and requirements of the masses and circumstances that the government can formulate policies on agriculture, social welfare, industry, education, health, defence, foreign affairs, science and technology and so on and so forth. The policies are goal oriented and meant to induce some change in the society. There are certain limitations of the policies in exercising its affects on the conditions in the society. The limitations of the public policy to that effect have been summarised by Thomas R. Dye as such (Dye, 1981) :

1. Some Societal problems are incapable solution because of the way in which they are defined. If problems are defined in relative rather than absolute terms, they may never be resolved by public policy. For example, if the poverty line is defined as the line which places one fifth of the population below it, then poverty will always be with us regardless of how well off the poor may become. Relative disparities in society may never be eliminated. Even if income differences among classes were tiny, then tiny differences may come to have great symbolic importance, and the problem of inequality may remain.[13]

2. Expectations may always outrace the capabilities of governments progress in any policy area may simply result in an upward movement in expectations about what policy should accomplish.

3. Policies that solve the problems of one group in society may create problems for other groups. In a plural society one man's solution may be another man's problem. For example, solving the problem of inequality in society may mean redistributive tax and spending policies which take from persons of above average wealth to give to persons with below average wealth. The latter may view this as a solution, but the former may view this as creating serious problems. There are no policies which can simultaneously attain mutually exclusive ends.[14]

4. It is quite possible that some societal forces cannot be harnessed by governments, even if it is desirable to do so. Governments may be unable to forcibly remove children from disadvantaged environments because of family objections even if this proves to be the only way to ensure equality of opportunity, and so on governments may not be able to bring about some societal changes.[15]

5. Frequently people adopt themselves to public policies in ways that render the policies useless. For example, we may solve the problem of poverty by government guarantees of a high annual income, but by doing we may reduce incentives

to work and thus swell the number of dependent families beyond the fiscal capacities of government to provide guarantees. Of course, we do not really know the impact of income guarantees on the work behaviour of the poor, but the possibility exists that adaptive behaviour may frustrate policy.[16]

6. Societal problems may have multiple causes, and a specific policy may be able to eradicate the problem. For example job training may not affect the hard core unemployed if their employ ability is also affected by chronic poor health.

7. The solution to some problems may require policies that are more costly than the problems. For example, it may turn out that certain levels of public disorder, including riots, civil disturbances, and occasional violence, cannot be eradicated without the adoption of very repressive policies, the forceable break-up of revolutionary parties, restrictions on public appearances of demagogues, the suppression of hate literature, the addition of large numbers of security forces, and so on. But these repressive policies would prove too costly interms of democratic values, freedom of speech and press, rights of assembly, freedom to form opposition parties. Thus a certain level of disorder may be the price we pay for democracy. Doubtless are other examples of societal problems that are simply too costly to solve.[17]

8. The political system is not structured for completely, rational decision making. The solution of societal problems generally implies a rational model, but government may not be capable of formulating policy in rational fashion. Instead the political system may reflect group interests, elite preferences, environmental forces, or incremental change, more than rationalism. Presumably, a democratic system is structured to reflect mass influences, whether these are rational or not. Elected officials respond to the demands of their constituents, and may inhibit completely rational approaches to public policy. Social science information does not exist to find policy solution even if there are solutions. Moreover, even where such information exists, it may find its way into the political arena.[18]

REFERENCES

1. Weiss, Carol, Evaluating Action Programmes : Readings in Social Action and Education, Boston, Allyn and Bacon, 1972.
2. Frohock, Fred M., Public Policy : Scope and Logic, Englewood Cliffs, Prentice Hall, 1979.
3. Policy evaluation is nothing but to know the policy impact in actuality or reality.
4. This is a definition defined by Prof. Lasswell in his book 'Who Gets What, When and How.'
5. Wholey, Joseph S., Federal Evaluation Policy, Washington, Urban Institute, 1970.
6. Wholey, Joseph S., *Ibid., op.cit.*
7. Appleby, "Policy and Administration", p. 7.
8. E.N. Gladden, "Essentials of Public Administration", Chap. V. Equity means equal treatment to all and uprightness.
9. Nachmias, David, Public Policy Evaluation, New York, St. Martin's Press, 1979.
10. Policies made by the government should be in accordance to the public interests, otherwise people will revolt against the government.
11. Dye, Thomas R., Understanding Public Policy, Englewood Cliffs, Prentice Hall, 1981.
12. Almond Gabriel A., Powell, G.B., Comparative Politics : A Development Approach, New Delhi, Amerind Publishing Co., 1975.
13. Dye Thomas, R., *op. cit.*
14. Hatry, Harry P., Winnie, Richard E., Fisk, Donald, M., Practical Programme Evaluation, Washington, Urban Institute, 1973.
15. Lippman, Water, Cf. Sorauf, Frank J., "The Public Interest Reconsidered", Journal of Politics, 1957.
16. Redford, Emmette S., Ideal and Practice in Public Administration, Tuscaloosa, University of Albama Press, 1958.
17. Wilson, James Q., "On Pettigrew and Armor", The Public Interest, 1973.
18. Dye, Thomas R., *op. cit.*

BIBLIOGRAPHY

Adorno, T.W. (*et al.*), The Authoritarian Personality, New York, Harper and Brothers, 1950.

Agger, Robert E. (*et al.*), The Rulers and the Ruled, New York, John Wiley and Sons, 1964.

Airan, J.W., T. Barnabas, and A.B. Shah (*eds.*), Changing a Wall of Glass, Bombay, P.C. Manaktala & Sons., 1965.

Aiyar, S.P. (ed.), Perspective on the Welfare State, Bombay, P.C. Manaktala & Sons, 1966.

Aiyar, S.P., and R. Srinivasan (eds.), Studies in Indian Democracy, Bombay, Allied Publishers, 1965.

Allison Graham, Essence of Decision, Boston, Little and Brown, 1971.

Almond, Gabriel A., "Comparative Political Systems", Journal of Politics, 1956.

Almond, Grabriel A., "A Comparative Study of Interest Groups and the Political Process", American Political Science Review, 1958.

Almond, Gabriel A., The Politics of Developing Nations, Princeton N.J., Princeton University Press, 1960.

Almond, Gabriel A., and G.B. Powell Jr., Comparative Politics : A Developmental Approach, Massachusetts, Little and Brown, 1973.

Anderson, Jack, "A Blueprint for Recreation", Washington Post 1974.

Anderson, James E., "Public Economic Policy and the Problem of Compliance : Notes for Research", Houston Law Review, 1966.

Anderson, James E., Public Policy Making, New York, Holt Rinehart and Winston, 1979.

Anderson, Walt (ed.), Politics and the Environment, California, Goodyear, 1975.

Apter, David, "A Comparative Method for the Study of Politics", American Journal of Sociology, 1958.

Apter, David E., The Politics of Modernization, Chicago, University of Chicago Press, 1965.

Aristotle, Politics, Translation by Rackman, London, Heinemann, 1932.

Armour, David, "The Double Double Standard", The Public Interest, 1973.

Arrow Kenneth, Social Change and Individual Values, New York, John Wiley and Sons, 1966.

Arrow, Kenneth, "Values and Collective Decision Making", in Laslett, Peter, and W.G. Runcimen (*eds.*), Philosophy, Politics and Society, Oxford, Basil Blackwell, 1969.

Awasthy, G.C., Broadcasting in India Bombay, Allied Publishers, 1965.

Bachrach, Peter, and The Theory of Democratic Elitism : A Critique, Boston, Little and Brown, 1967.

Bachrach, Peter, and Morton Baratz, "Decisions and Non-decisions", American Political Science Review, 1963.

Bachrach, Peter and Morton Baratz, Power and Poverty, New York Oxford University Press, 1979.

Ball, A.R., Modern Politics and Government, London, MacMillan, 1971.

Barry, Brian, Political Argument, New York, Humanities Press 1965.

Basil Blackwell Locke : The Second Treatise of Government, Korwich Fletcher and Son., 1976.

Bauer, Raymond A., and Kenneth J. Gergen (eds.), The Study of Policy Formulation, New York, Free Press, 1968.

Bauer Raymond A. (*et al.*), American Business and Public Policy, Chicago Aldine, 1972.

Bay, Christian, The Structure of Freedom, Stanford, Stanford University Press, 1958.

Beer, "Pressure Groups and Parties in Britain", American Political Science Review, 1956.

Beer and Ulma, Patterns of Government, New York, Random House, 1962.

Bent, Alan Edward, the Politics of Law Enforcement, Lexington, D.C. Heath and Co., 1974.

Bentley, Arthur, The Process of Government, Evanston Principia Press, 1949.

Berger, Raoul, Executive Privilege, A Constitutional Myth, Cambridge Harvard University Press, 1974.

Bremen Davied, It is So Ordered, New York, Norton, 1966.

Bensten Carl, and Bobb Wooword, All The President's, Men, New York, Warnar, 1975.

Bhaskaran, R., Sociology of Politics, Bombay, Asia Publishing House, 1967.

Bickel, Alexander, The Least Dangerous Branch, New York, Boobs–Merrill, 1960.

Binner, Paul R., Quoted in Franklin, Jack L. and J.H. Thrasser, An Introduction to Programme Evaluation, New York, Johnwiley and Sons, 1976.

Blalock, H., and A. Blalock, "Towards a Clarification of System Analysis in the Social Sciences", Philosophy of Science, 1959.

Blondel, Jr., An Introduction to Comparative Governments, London, Weldenfield and Nicholson, 1969.

Bombwall, K.R., and L.P., Choudhary (eds.), Aspects of Democratic Government and Politics in India, Delhi, Atma Ram & Sons, 1968.

Booms, Bernard H., and James R. Halldorson, "The Politics of Redistribution : A Reformulation", American Political Science Review, 1973.

Bones James T., "The absence of Knowledge of Distributional Impacts : An Obstacle to Effective Policy Analysis and Decisions", in Hanmen Robert H., and Julius Margolis (eds.), Public Expenditure and Policy Analysis, Chicago, Markham , 1970.

Brams, Steve, Game Theory and Politics, New York, Free Press, 1975.

Braybrooks, David and Charles Lindblom, A Strategy of Decision, New York, Free Press, 1963.

Brecht, Arnold, Political Theory, Princeton N. J., Princeton University Press, 1959.

Breackenridge, A.C., The Executive Press, Nebraska, University of Nebraska, Press, 1974.

Buchanan, James, and Gordon Tullock, The Calculus of Consent, Michigan, University of Michigan Press, 1960.

Buckley, Walter (ed), Modern Systems Research for the Behavioural Scientist, Chicago, Aldine, 1968.

Burke, Edmund, Thoughts the Causes of the Present Discontent, 1970.

Calin Edmond, The Moral Decision, Bloomington, Indiana University Press, 1959.

Campbell, Angus (*et al.*), The Voter Decides, Evanston, Row and Peterson, 1954.

Campbell Angus, Elections and the Political Order, New York, Johnwiley and Sons, 1966.

Cantril, Hadley, The Pattern of Human Concerns, New Jersy, Rutgers University Press, 1965.

Caputo David A., Urban America : The Policy Alternatives, San Francisco, W.H. Freeman & Co., 1976.

Caputo, David A., Urban America : The Policy Alternatives, San Francisco, W.H. Freeman & Co., 1977.

Casper Jonathan D., "The Supreme Court and National Policy Making", American Politic Science Review, 1976.

Chamberlain, John, "Provision of Collective Goods as a Function of Groups Size", American Political Science Review, 1974.

Chambers, William N., and W.O. Burnham (eds.), The American Party Systems : Stage of Political Development, New York, 1967.

Chatterjee, N.C., "Good Government", Free Press Journal, January 1966.

Cheluva Raju, "Governmental Planning in India–Development, Nature and Goals", Mysore University Journal, March 1962.

Chin, Y.L., The Political Theory of Thomas Hill Green, New York, 1967.

Churchman, C. West, The Systems Approach, New York, Dell, 1968.

Clark Kenneth B., Dark Ghetto, New York, Harper and Row, 1965.

Clark Terry N., Community Structure and Decision-Making : Comparative Analysis San Francisco, Chandler Publishing Company, 1968.

Clinard, Marshall B., Sociology of Deviant Behaviour, New York, Holt Rinehart and Winston, 1957.

Cob, Roger W., and Charles E. Elder, Participation in American Politics : The Dynamics of Agenda Building, Boston Allyn and Bacon, 1972.

Coker, F. W., Recent Political Thought, Calcutta, World Press, 1966.

Coleman, James, "Problems of Conceptualization and Measurement in Studying Political Impact", In Bolbeare, Kenneth (ed.), Public Policy Evaluation Revelry Hills, Sage Publications, 1975.

Commoner, Barry, The Closing Circle, New York, 1971.

Connolly, William, Political Science and Ideology, New York, Atherton Press, 1967.

Connolly William (ed.), Social Structure and Political Theory, Lexington, D.C. Heath, 1974.

Cannolly, William, The Terms of Political Discourse, Lexington, D.C. Heath, 1974.

Crecine, John P., Governmental Problem Solving, Chicago, Rand McNally, 1969.

Crozier, Michael, The Bureaucratic Phenomenon, Chicago, University of Chicago Press, 1963.

Cutright, Philips, "National Political Developments : Its Measurement and Social Correlates", in Polsby Nelson (*et al.*) Politics and Social Life, Boston, Houghton Mifflin Company, 1963.

Dahl, Robert A., Who Governs, New Haven, Yale University Press, 1961.

Dahl, Robert A., "Decision-Making in Democracy : The Supreme Court as a National Policy Maker", in Shapiro Martin (*ed.*), The Supreme Court and Public Policy, Glenview, Scott-Foresman, 1969.

Dahl, Robert A., Modern Political Analysis, New Delhi, Prentice Hall, 1978.

Dahl, Robert A., and Charles E. Lindblom, Politics, Economic and Welfare, New York, Harper and Row, 1953.

Dahl, Robert A., and Edward R. Tufte, "Further Reflections on The Elitist, Theory of Democracy", American Political Science, Review, 1966.

Dahl, Robert A., and Edward R. Tufte, Size and Democracy, Stanford, Standford University Press, 1974.

Daniels, Jonathen Frontiers on the Potomac, New York, MacMillan, 1946.

Davis, J. Clearence, The Politics of Pollution, Indiana—Polis, Bobbs-Merrill, 1975.

Davis, Kenneth C., Discretionary Justice, Baton Rouge, Louisiana Stage University Press.

Davis Morton R., and V.A. Lewis, Models of Political Systems, Delhi Vikas, 1971.

Davis, Otto A. (*et al.*), "A Theory of Budgetary Process", American Political Science Review, 1966.

Dean, Horward J., Judicial Review and Democracy, New York, 1966.

Dester, I.M., Presidents, Bureaucrats and Foreign Policy, New Jersey, Princeton University Press, 1972.

Deutsch, Karl W., Politics and Government, Boston, Houghton Mifflin, 1974.

Devlin, Patrick, The Enforcement of Morals, Oxford, Oxford University Press, 1965.

Dewley, John, The Public and Its Problem, New York, 1972.

Dexter, Lewis Anthony, American Business and Public Policy, New York, Atherton Press, 1964.

Donovan, John C., The Policy Makers, New York, Pegasus, 1970.

Dorfman Robert, Measuring Benefit of Government Investment, Washington D.C., Brookings Institution, 1965.

Dorothy, Fosdick, What is Liberty? A Study in Political Theory, New York, 1939.

Dorsen, Norman and Stephen Gillers, None of your Business : Government Secrecy in America, New York, Penguin Books, 1974.

Downs, Anthony, An Economic Theory of Democracy, New York, Harper and Row, 1957.

Dror, Yehezkal, Public Policy Reexamined, Scranton, Chandler, 1968.

Dye, Thomas R., Politics Economic and the Public : Policy Outcomes in Fifty States, Chicago, Rand MacNally, 1966.

Dye Thomas R., "Inequality and Civil Rights Policy in the States", Journal of Politics, 1969.

Dye, Thomas R., and Harmon Zeigler, The Irony of Democracy, California, Wadsworth, 1970.

Dye, Thomas R., Policy Analysis Alabama, University of Alabama Press, 1976.

Dye, Thomas R., and Virginia Gray, Determinents of Public Policy, Boston, Lexington, 1980.

Dye, Thomas R., Understanding Public Policy, New Jersy, Prentice Hall, 1981.

Easton, David, The Political System, New York, Knopf, 1953.

Easton, David, "An Approach to the Analysis of Political Systems", World Politics, 1957.

Easton, David, A Framework of Political Analysis, Engewood Cliffs, New Jersy, Prentice Hall, 1965.

Easton, David, A system Analysis of Political Life, New York, John Wiley and Sons, 1965.

Eckstein, Harry, Division and Cohesion in Democracy, Princeton, Princeton University Press, 1966.

Eckstein, Harry, "Authority Patterns : A Structural Basis for Political Inquiry," American Political Science Review, 1973.

Eckstein, Harry, and Ted Robert Gurr, Patterns of Authority, New York, Wiley International, 1975.

Edelman, Murray, The Symbolic Use of Politics, Urbana University of Illinois Press, 1964.

Edinger, Lewis, Political Leadership in Industrialized Societies : Studies in Comparative Analysis, New York, John Wiley and Sons, 1967.

Edward Geroge C., and Ira Sharkansky, The policy Predicament San Francisco, Freeman, 1978.

Ehrmann, Henry Interest Groups on Four Continents, Pittsburgh University of Pittsburgh Press, 1958.

Elazer Danial J., American Federalism : A View from the State, New York, Crowell, 1976.

Encyclopedia Britannica, Volume 14, Chicago, Helen Hemingmay Beton, 1973.

Erickson Maynard L., and Jack P. Gibbs,"The Deterrence Question", Social Science Quarterly, 1973.

Erickson, Robert S., and Norman R. Luttbeg, American Public Opinion, New York, John Wiley and Sons, 173.

Espstein, Edward Jay, News From Nowhere, New York, Random House, 1973.

Etzioni Amitai, A Comparative Analysis of Complex Organizations Glencoe, Illinois, Free Press, 1961.

Etzioni Amitai, Modern Organizations, New Jersy, Prentic Hall, 1964.

Etzioni, Amitai, The Active Society, New York, Free Press, 1968.

Eulau, Heinz (*et al.*), Political Behaviour, New York, Free Press, 1956.

Eulau, Heinz, and Kenneth Prewitt Labyrinths of Democracy : Adaptations, Linkages, Representation and Policies in Urban Politics, Indianapolis, Bobb-Merrill, 1973.

Eyestone, Robert, The Threads of Public Policy : A Study in Policy Leadership, Indianapolis, Bobb-Merril, 1971.

Fabricant, Soloman, Trend of Government Activity in the United States Since 1900, New York, National Bureau of Economic Research, 1952.

Feagin Joe, Subordinating the Poor, New Jersy, Prentice Hall, 1975.

Fenno, Richard F, Jr., The Power of the Purse, Boston, Little Brown and Company, 1966.

Fenno, Richard F. Jr., Congressmen in Committees, Boston, Little Brown and Company, 1973.

Fenton, John H., People and Parties in Politics, Illinois, Foresman, 1966.

Ferejohn, John, Pork Barrel Politics, California, Stanford University Press, 1974.

Festinger, Leon, A Theory of Cognitive Dissonance, California Standford University Press, 1957.

Finer, H., Theory and Practice of Modern Government, New York, Methuen, 1962.

Fisher, Thomas C., "Defunis in the Supreme Court : Is That All There Is ?" The Journal of Law and Education, 1975.

Fisher, Glenn F., "Interstate Variation in State and Local Government Expenditure", National Tax Journal, March 1964.

Fisher, John C., Energy Crisis in Perspective, John Wiley and Sons, 1974.

Fishburn, Peter, "Paradoxes of Voting", American Political Science Review, 1974.

Flathman, Richard, The Public Interest, New York, John Wiley and Sons, 1966.

Ford, Franklin L., Robe and Sword, Cambridge, Harward University Press, 1953.

Ford Foundation, Exploring Energy Choices, 1974.

Fortas Abe, "The Case Against Capital Punishment", The New York Times Magazine, January, 23, 1977.

Fox, Irwing K., and Orris C., Hanfindahl, "Attainment of Efficiency in Satisfying Demands for Water Resources, American Economic Review, May 1964.

Franklen, Joseph, The Making of Foreign Policy : An Analysis of Decision Making, New York, Oxford University Press, 1963.

Freeman, J. Leiper, The Political Process, New York, Random House 1965.

Frejka Tomes, "The Prospects for a Stationary World Population", Scientific American, March, 1973.

Friedrich, Carl J., Man and His Government, New York, MacGraw Hill, 1963.

Fritschler, A. Lee, Smoking and Politics, New Jersy, Prentice Hall, 1975.

Frohock Fred M., "Notes on the Concept of Politics", The Journal of Politics, 1974.

Frohock Fred M., Normative Political Theory, New Jersy, Prentice Hall 1974

Frohock Fred M., "The Structure of Politics", American Political Science Review, 1978.

Frohock, Fred M., Public Policy : Scope and Logic, New Jersy, Prentice Hall, 1979.

Frolich, Norman, Joe A. Oppenheimer, and Oran R. Young, Political Leadership and Collective Goods, New Jersy, Prentice Hall, 1973.

Froman, Lewis A., People and Politis. New Jercy, Prentice Hall, 1962.

Froman Erich, Escape from Freedom, New York, Farrer and Rinehart, 1941.

Fry, Brayan R., and Richard F. Winters, "The Politics of Redistribution", American Political Science Review, 1970.

Galbraith, John Kenneth, The New Industrial State, Boston Houghton Mufflin, 1967.

Galbraith, John Kenneth, The New Industrial State, Boston.

Galensen, Walter (ed.), Comparative Labour Movements, New Jersy, Prentice Hall, 1952.

Gallucci, Robert L., Neither Peace nor Honor, Baltimore, John Hopkins University Press, 1975.

Gamson, William, Power and Discontent, Illinois, The Dorsey Press, 1968.

Gardner, Judy, "Kissing Retains Principle Role in Foreign Policy", Congressional Quarterly Weekly Report, 1975.

George, Theodore and Roger, D. Hansen, the Role of Information in Decision-Making on Foreign Aid", in Banner R.A., and K.J. Georgian (eds)., The Study of Policy Formulation, New York, Free Press, 1968.

George, Alexander L., and Juliette L. George, Woodrow Wilson and Colonel House : A Personality Study, New York, John Day, 1956.

George, Alexander L., "The Case for Multiple Advocacy in Making Foreign Policy", American Political Science Review, 1972.

Gadgil, D.R., Planning and Economic Policy in India, Bombay, Asia Publishing House, 1961.

Gadre, Kamala, Indian Way to Socialism, New Delhi,Vir Publishing House, 1966.

Ghosh, O.K., Problem of Economic Planning in India, Allahabad, Kitabistan, 1957.

Ghósh, S., "A Welfare State For India And Democracy", in Tiwari S.C., and S.R. Sharma (eds.), Political Studies, Agra, S.L. Agarwala and Co., 1966.

Gibbs, Jack P., "Crime, Punishment, and Deterrence", Social Science Quarterly, 1968.

Gibson, Quentin, "Power", Philosophy of Social Science, 1971.

Gibson, Frank K., "A Path Analytic Treatment of Corrections Output", Social Science Quarterly, 1973.

Gilbert, G.M., The Psychology of Dictatorship, New York, The Donald Press Company, 1950.

Gilmour, Robert S., "Environmental Preservation and Politics", Political Science Quarterly, 1976.

Gilpin, Robert, American Scientists and Nuclear Weapons Policy, New Jersy, Princeton University Press, 1962.

Ginsberg, Benjamin, "Elections and Public Policy", American Political Science Review, 1976.

Goodnow Frank J., Politics and Administration, New York, Russell and Russell, 1960.

Golden, Joseph C., Truth is the First Casuality, Chicago, Rand McNally, 1969.

Gramlich, Edward M., and Patrician P., Koshall, Educational Performance Contracting, Washington D.C., Brooking Institution, 1975.

Gray, Virginia, "Innovations in the States", American Political Science Review, 1973.

Gray, Virginia, "Models of Comparative State Politics : A Comparison of Cross Sectional and Time Series Analysis", American Journal of Political Science, 1976.

Gray, David L., The Supreme Court and the News Media, Illinois, Northwestern University Press, 1968.

Grodzing, Morton, The Loyal and the Disloyal Chicago, University of Chicago Press, 1956.

Gross, Bertram (ed.), Social Intelligence for America's Future, Boston, Allyn and Bacon, 1969.

Gross, Bertram, "The New System Budgeting", Public Administration Review, 1969.

Gross, Lewellyn (ed.), Symposium of Sociological Theory, New York, Harper and Row, 1959.

Grumm, John G., "The Analysis of Policy Impact", in Greenstein Fred. I., and Nelson W. Polsby (eds.), Policies and Policymaking, Volume 6 of the Handbook of Political Science, Massachusetts, Addison Wesley, 1975.

Gulley, Halbert E., Discussion, Conference and Group Process, New York, Holt, Rinehart and Winston, 1968.

Gupta, Ranjit, Planning for Self-Reliance, New Delhi, Implex India 1966.

Gurr Ted, Why Men Rebel, New Jersy, Priceton University Press, 1970.

Gusfield, Joseph R., "Mass Society and Extremist Politics", American Sociological Review, 1962.

Guttsman, W.L., The British Political Elite, New York, Basic Books, 1963.

Gwyn, William B., and George C. Edwards, Perspectives on Public Policy-Making, New Orleans, Tulane Studies in Political Science, 1975.

Halberstam, David, The Best and the Brightest, New York, Random House, 1972.

Halperin, Morton H., Bureaucratic Politics and Foreign Policy Washington D.C., Brookings Institution, 1974.

Haltzman, Abraham, Interest Groups and Lobbying, London, MacMillan, 1966.

Hanke, Steve H., and Richard A. Walker, "Benefit—Cost Analysis Reconsidered", Water Resource Research, 1974.

Hansan, Susan B., "Participation, Political Structure and Concurrence", American Political Science Review, 1975.

Hare, R.M., Freedom and Reason, New York, Oxford University Press, 1965.

Harrison, Martin, Trade Unions in Labour Party Since 1945, London, George Allen and Unwin, 1960.

Harrison Ross, "No Paradox in Democracy", Political Studies 1970.

Harsanvi, John, "Can the Maximin Principle serve as a Basis for Morality ?" American Political Science Review, 1975.

Hart, H.L.A., Law, Liberty, and Morality, New York, Vintage Books, 1963.

Hart, H.L.A., The Concept of Law, London, Oxford University Press, 1961.

Hatry, Harry P. (*et al.*), Practical Programme Evaluation, Washington D.C., Urban Institute, 1973.

Haveman, Robert H., The Economic Performance of Public Investments, Baltimore, Johns Hopkins University Press, 1972.

Haveman Robert H., and Julius Margolis (eds.) Public Expenditure and Policy Analysis, Chicago, Markham, 1970.

Hayek Frederick A., The Road to Serfdom Chicago, University of Chicago Press, 1944.

Heard, Alexander, The Costs of Democracy, Chapel Hill, University of North Carolina, 1960.

Heckscher, Gunnar, The Study of Comparative Government and Politics, New York, MacMillan, 1957.

Heclo, Hugh, "Policy Analysis", British Journal of Political Science, 1972.

Heidenheimer Arnold (*et al.*), Comparative Public Policy, New York, St. Martin's Press, 1975.

Heilbroner, Robert A. An inquiry into Human Prospect, New York, Norton, 1974.

Hold, Virginia, The Public Interest and Individual Interests, New York, Basic Books, 1970.

Herring Pendleton, "On the Study of Government", American Political Science Review, 1953.

Hess, Robert D., and David Easton, The Child's Changing Image of the President", Public Opinion Quarterly, 1960.

Hicks, J. R., A Revision of Demand Theory, Oxford, Oxford University Press, 1956.

Hilsman, Roger, To Mone a Nation, Garden City, Double-Day and Company, 1967.

Hinderaker, Ivon, Party Politics, New York, Henry Holt and Company, 1956.

Hirschman, Albert O., Journeys Towards Progress, New York, The Twentieth Century Fund, 1963.

Hoebel, Adamson, The Law of Primitive Man, Cambridge Harvard University Press, 1954.

Hofferbert, Rischard I., "Ecological Development and Policy Change in the American States", Midwest Journal of Political Science, 1966.

Holden, Barry, The Nature of Democracy, New York, Harper and Row, 1974.

Holden, Mathew, and Denies L. Dresang, Sage Year Book in Politics and Public Policy, Volume 1, Beverly Hills, California, 1975.

Hook, Sydney, (ed.), Human Values and Economic Policy, New York, New York University Press, 1967.

Hopkins, Anne H., Public Opinion and Support for Policy in American States", American Journal of Political Science, 1974.

Howard J. Woodford, "On the Fludity of Judicial Choice", American Political Science Review, 1968.

Hyman, Herbert H. (*et al.*), Application of Methods of Evaluations Berkeley, University of California Press, 1962.

Iengar H.U.R., Business and Planned Economy, Bombay, Vora and Co., 1968.

Jain R.B., "Legislative Role Differentiation in Contemporary Societies Journal of Parliamentary Information, New Delhi, 1975.

Jacob, Herbert, and Kenneth N. Vines (eds.), Politics in the American States, Boston, Little Brown and Company, 1971.

Janowitz, Morris, The Military in the Political Development of the New Nations, Chicago, University of Chicago Press, 1964.

Jeffry, Richard C., The Logic of Decision, New York McGraw–Hill, 1965.

Jennings, M. Kent, Community Influentials : A Study of Elites, New York, Free Press, 1964.

John V.V., Education and Language Policy, Bombay Noehiketa Publishers, 1969.

Johnson John J., The Role of Military in Underdeveloped Countries, Princeton, Princeton University Press, 1962.

Jones, Charles, O., An Introduction to the Study of Public Policy, Belmont, Prentice Hall, 1968.

Jenoes Charles O., Clean Air : The Policies and Politics of Pollution Control, Pittsburgh University of Pittshurgh Press.

Jenes, M.H., Executive Decision Making, Illinios, Richard D. Irvin, 1964.

Kalin, Harman, On Thermonuclear War, New Jersy, Perception University Press, 1961.

Kalin, Herman, Thinking about Unthinkable, New York, Horizon Press,1962.

Kanfman, Herbert, Administrative Feedback : Monitoring Subordinates Behaviour, Washington D.C., Brookings Institution, 1973.

Kaplan Abraham, American Ethics and Public Policy, New York, Oxford University Press. 1963.

Kariel, Henry S., The Promise of Politics, New Jersy, Practice Hall, 1966.

Karist, Kenneth L., and Harold W. Horowitz, "Affirmative Actions and Equal Protection", Virginia Law Review, 1974.

Kass Leon R., "Regarding the End of Medicine and the Pursuit of Health", The Public Interest, 1975.

Katz, Elihu, and Pant F. Lazarsfeld, Personal Influence, New York, Free Press, 1955.

Kearns, Doris, Lyndon Johnson and the American Dream, New York, Harper and Row, 1976.

Keech, William R., "Electoral Politics and the Meaning of Partnership in Federal Minimum Wage Policy", (Paper presented on September 4, 1975 at the Annual Meeting of the American Political Science Association held at San Francisco.

Keech, William R., and James W. Prothbro, "American Government", Journal of Politics, 1968.

Kelley George A. (ed.), Government Aid to Non-Public Schools, Yes or No? New York, St. John's University Press, 1972.

Kent, Frank, Political Behaviour : The Heretofore Unwritten Laws, Customs and Principles of Politics as Practical in the United States, New York, William Morrow and Company, 1928.

Kent, Frank, The Great Game of Politics, Garden City, New York, Doubleday, Doran and Company, 1935.

Kent, James K., "The Coleman Report : Opening Pandora's Box", Phidelta Kappan, January 1968.

Kershaw, David and Jerelyn Fair (eds.), "Final Report of the New Jersy Graduated Work Incentive Experiment", University of Wisconsin, Institute for Research on Poverty, 1974.

Kershaw, Joseph A., Government against Poverty, Chicago Markham, 1970.

Key, V.O. Jr., American State Politics : An Introduction, New York, Knopf., 1956.

Key V.O., Jr., New England State Politics, Princeton, New Jersy Princeton University Press, 1959.

Key, V.O. Jr., Public Opinion and American Democracy, New York, Knopf., 1967.

King, Anthony, "Ideas Institutions and Policies of Governments : A Comparative Analysis", British Journal of Political Science, 1973.

King Martin Luther, "Letter From Brimingham Jail", in Lynd Staughton (ed.), Nonviolence in America : A Documentary History Indianapolis, Bobbs-Merrill, 1966.

Kingdom, John W., Congressmen's Voting Decision, New York, Harper and Row, 1973.

Krichheimer, Otto, Political Justice, New York, Princeton University Press, 1961.

Kissinger, Henry, Nuclear Weapons and Foreign Policy, New York, Council on Foreign Relations, 1957.

Kissinger Henry A. (ed.), Problems of National Strategy, New York, Praeger, 1965.

Kleck, Gray, "Capital Punishment, Gun Ownership, and Homicide American Journal of Sociology, 1979.

Kneese, Allen W., and Charles Schultz, Pollution Prices and Public Policy, Washington D.C., Brookings Institutions, 1975.

Kohler, Heinz, Welfare and Planning, New York, John Wiley and Sons, 1966.

Kohlmeier, Louis J., The Regulators, New York, Harper and Row, 1969.

Kraft, Joseph, "School for Statesmen", Harper's, July, 1958.

Krasnow, Erwing G., and Lawrence D. Langlay, The Politics of Broadcast Regulation, New York, St., Martin's Press, 1978.

Krause, Walter, Economic Development, Belmont, Wadswarth, 1961.

Krislow, Samuel, The Supreme Court in the Political Process, New York, MacMillan 1965.

Kristol, Irwing, "Social Indicators Reports and Accounts", The Annals, 1970.

Kuznets, Simon, Modern Economic Growth, New Haven, Yale University Press, 1966.

Ladd, Bruce, Crisis in Credibility, New York, American Library, 1968.

Fafaver, John D., "Zero-Base Budgeting in New Mexico", State Government, 1974.

Landau, M., "On the Basis of Metaphor in Political Analysis", Social Research, 1961.

Lane, Robert E., Political Ideology, New York, Free Press, 1962.

Lane, Robert, and David Sears, Public Opinion, Englewood Cliffs, New Jersy, Prentice Hall, 1904 .

Lapalombara, Joseph, Interest Groups in Italian Politics, Princeton, Princeton University Press, 1964.

Lasswell, Harold D., The Political Writings of Harold D. Lasswell, Illinois, Free Press, 1951.

Lasswell, Harold D., The Decision Process, Madison, University of Maryland, 1956.

Lasswell, Harold D., and Abraham Kaplan, Power and Society, New Haven, Yale University Press, 1970.

Lathem, Earl, The Group Basis of Politics, New York, Cronell University Press, 1952.

Lazarsfeld, Pant F. (*et al.*), The People's Choice, New York, Duell, Sloan and Pearoe 1944.

Lazin, Frederick A., "The Failure of Federal Enforcement of Civil Rights Regulations in Public Housing, 1963–1971 : The Cooperation of Federal Agency by its Local Constituency, Policy Sciences, 1973.

Le Breton, Edmond, "114 Billoin in Tax Breaks", New Orleans, Times Pleayune, 1977.

Leighton, Alexander, The Governing Men, Princeton, Princeton University Press, 1945.

Leites, Nathan, On the Games of Politics in Frances, Stanford, Stanford University Press, 1959.

Lenbsdorf, Carl P., "Kennedy Tells of Envoy Cable", Now Orlean Times, Plcayune, 1974.

Lengle, James, L., and Byron Shafer, "Primary Rules, Political Power and Social Change", American Political Science Review, 1976.

Lenthol, David A., Electioneering in Democracy, New York, John Wiley and Sons, 1968.

Lerner, Daniel, The Passing of Traditional Society, New York, Free Press, 1958.

Lerner, Daniel and Harold D. Lasswell (eds.), The Policy Sciences, Stanford, Stanford University Press, 1960.

Leving, Betsy (ed.),"Future Direction for School Finance Reform", A Symposium in Law and Contemporary Problems, U.S.A., Vol. 38, 1974.

Levin, Betsy," Recent Developments in Law and Equal Education Opportunity, U.S.A., Journal of Law and Education, 1975.

Levine, Robert A., The Poor Ye Need Not Have with You : Lessons from the War of Poverty, Cambridge, MIT Press, 1970.

Levy, Leonard W., Judicial Review and the Supreme Court, New York, Harper and Row, 1967.

Levy Marion, The Structure of Society, Princeton, Princeton University Press, 1952.

Lewin, Kent, Resolving Social Conflict, New York, Harper and Brothers, 1948.

Lewis—Beck, Michael, "The Relative Importance of Socio-Economic Variables and Political Variables in Public Policy", American Political Science Review, 1977.

Lewis, Frank, L., and Frank G. Zarb, "Federal Programme Evaluation from the OMB Perspective", USA, Public Administration Review, 1974.

Lindblom, Charles E., "The Science of Muddling Through", USA., Public Administration Review, 1959.

Lindblom, Chalres E., The Intelligence of Democracy, New York, Free Press, 1965.

Lindblom, Charles E., The Policy Making Process, Englewood Cliffs, Prentice Hall, 1969.

Lindquist, Robert E., and Arthur E. Wise, "Developments in Education Litigation : Equal Protection, USA., Journal of Law and Education, 1976.

Lineberry, Robert L., and Ira Sharkansky, Urban Politics and Public Policy, New York, Harper and Row, 1974.

Lineberry, Robert L., and Edmund D. Fowler, "Reformism and Public Policies in American Cities, American Political Science Review, 1967.

Lineberry, Robert L., American Public Policy : What Government Does and What Difference it Makes, New York, Harper and Row, 1977.

Lippnam Walter, Cf. Sorauf, Frank J., "The Public Interest Reconsidered, U.S.A., Journal of Politics, 1957.

Lipset, Seymour Martin, Political Man, New York, Doubleday, 1963.

Lipset, Seymour Martin, Politics and Social Sciences, New York, Wiley, 1966.

Lipson, Leslie, The Democratic Civilization, New York, Oxford University Press, 1964.

Lockard, Duane, The Politics of State and Local Government, New York, MacMillan,1963.

Long, Norton E., "Public Policy and Administration : The Goal of Rationality and Responsibility", U.S.A., Public Administration Review, 1954.

Lowi, Theodore J., "American Business and Public Policy : Case Study and Political Theory", U.S.A., World Politics, 1964.

Lowi, Theodore, The End of Liberalism, New York, Norton, 1969.

Lubell, Samuel, The Future of American Politics, New York, Harper and Brothers, 1951.

Luce, R. Duncan and Howard Reufta, Games and Decisions, New York, John Wiley and Sons, 1967.

Luethy, Herbert, France Against Herself, New York, Meridian Books, 1957.

Kukes, Steven Power : A Radical View, Atlantic Highlands, New Jersy, Humanities Press, 1975.

Maass Arthur A., "Congress and Water Resources", American Political Science Review, 1950.

Maass, Arthur, Muddy Water, Cambridge, Harverd University Press, 1951.

Machiavelli, The Prince, Translation by Musa, Mark, New York, St. Martin's Press, 1964.

Machlup, Firtz. The Production and Distribution Knowledge in United States, Princeton, Princeton University Press, 1962.

Machpherson, C.B., The Real World of Democracy, Oxford, Oxford University, Press, 1972.

Machpherson, C.B., Democratic Theory : Essays in Retrieval, Oxford, Oxford University Press, 1973.

MacRae, Duncan, Dimensions of Congressional Voting, California, University of California Press, 1958.

Mahood, H.R., Pressure Groups in American Politics, New York, Charles Scribner's Sons, 1967.

Mair, Lucy, Primitive Government, Baltimore, Penguin Books, 1962.

Manley, John F., The Politics of Finance, Boston, Little and Brown, 1970.

March, John, and Herbert Simon, Organizations, New York, John Wiley and Sons, 1958.

March, J.G., Handbook of Organizations, Chicago, Rand McNally and Company, 1965.

Marcuse, Herbert, One Dimensional Man, Boston, Beacon Press, 1964.

Marglin, Stephen A., Public Investment Criteria, Cambridge, Massachusetts Institute of Technology, 1967.

Margolis Michael, "From Confusion to Confusion : Issues and the American Voter (1965-1972), American Political Science Review, 1977.

Markus, Gregory, "Electoral Coalitions and Senate Roll Call Behaviour : An Ecological Analysis", American Journal of Political Science, 1974.

Marmor, Theodore R., The Politics of Medicare, Chicago, Aldine, 1970.

Marshall Margaret H., "The Standard of Interest", USA, Journal of Law and Education, 1975.

Masani, M.R., Government Economic Policies, Mimeographed, (Author), 1962.

Masoti, Lewis and Donald Bowen (eds.), Riots and Rebellion, New York, Sage Publications, 1968.

Mathew, Jr. and Dennis L. Dresang (eds.), Sage Year Book in Politics and Public Policy, Volume 1, Beverly Hills, California, 1975.

Matthews, Donald R., and James A. Stimsoin Yeas and Nays : Normal Decision Making in the U.S. House of Representatives, New York, John Wiley and Sons 1975.

Maxey, Political Philosophies, London, 1964.

Mayhew, David, Party Loyalty among Congressmen, Cambridge, Harvard University, 1966.

Mayo, Henry, An Introduction to Democratic Theory, New York, Oxfor University Press, 1960.

Mazur, Allan, "Disputes Between Experts", USA, Minerva, 1973.

McCleod, J.M., L.B. Becker and J.E. Byrne, "Another Look at the Agenda-Setting Function of the Press", USA., Communications Research, April 1974.

McCleod, J.M., (*et al.*), "The Political Consequences of Agenda-Setting", USA., Mass Communication Review, 1976.

McClosky, Herbert, Paul J. Hoffman, and Rosemary O. Hara, "Consensus and Ideology in American Politics", American Political Science Review, 1964.

McCombs, Maxiwell E. and Donal L. Shaw, "The Agenda-Setting Function of the Mass Media", USA., Public Opinion Quarterly, 1972.

McCombs, M.E., "Agenda-Setting Research ; A Bibliographical Essays" USA., Political Communication Review, March, 1976.

McConnel, Grant, Private Power and American Democracy, New York, Knopf., 1966.

McGaffin, William and Erivin Knoll, Anything But the Truth, New York, Putnam's 1968.

McKean, Roland, Efficiency in Government Through Systems Analysis, New York, John Wiley and Sons, 1958.

McPherson, Harry, A Political Education, Boston, Little and Brown Company, 1972

Meadows, Donella (*et al.*), The Limits to Growth, New York, New American Library, 1972.

Meadows, Robert G., "Issue Emphasis and Public Opinion", USA., American Politics Quarterly, 1976.

Meier, K.J., "Representative Bureaucracy : An Empirical Analysis", American Political Science Review, 1975.

Meier, K.J., and L.G. Nigro, "Representative Bureaucracy and Policy Preferences : A Study in the Attitudes of Federal Executives", Paper presented at the Annual Meeting of the American Political Science Association held at San Francisco on September 4, 1975.

Mesarvic, M., and Edward Pestal, Making at the Turning Point, New York, American Library, 1974.

Miccory, Charles N.R., The Structure of Political Thought, London, McGraw-Hill, 1963.

Michels, Robert, Political Parties, London, Jarrold and Son, 1915.

Miller, Arthur S., "On the Choice of Major Premises in Supreme Court Opinions", USA, Journal of Public Law, 1965.

Miller, Arthur, and W. E., Miller, "Ideology in the 1972 Election : Myth or Reality—A Rejoinder", American Political Science Review, 1976.

Miller, The Nature of Politics, London Gereld Dickworth, 1962.

Miller and Stockes, "Constituency Influence in Congress", American Political Science Review, 1963.

Millikan, Marx. F. (ed.), Income Stabilization for a Developing Democracy, New Haven Yale University Press, 1953.

Milner, Neal A., The Court and Law Enforcement, California, Sage Publications, 1971.

Mills, Kay, "Public Dislikes for Regulatory Agencies Cited by Symposium", USA., New Orleans Times—Picayune, November 1975.

Mills, Nicholas (ed.), The Great School Bus Controversy, New York, Teachers College Press, 1973.

Mitchell, William, "Politics as the Allocation of Values : A Critique" USA., Ethics 71, January, 1961.

Mitchell, Joyce M., and William C. Mitchell Political Analysis and Public Policy, New Delhi, Thompson Press, 1972.

Mohr Lawrence B., "Determinations of Innovations in Organizations", American Political Science Review, 1969.

Morre Emily C., "Abortion and Public Policy : What are the Issues ?" USA., Law Forum, 1971.

Mosca, G., The Ruling Class, New York, McGraw-Hill, 1939.

Moynihan, Daniel Patrick, Maximum Feasible Misunderstanding : Community Action and War on Poverty, New York, Free Press, 1969.

Moynihan, Daniel Patrick, The Politics of Guaranteed Annual Income, New York, Vintage, 1973.

Mueller, Eva, "Public Attitude, Towards Fiscal Programmes", USA., The Quarterly Journal of Economics, May, 1963.

Munger, Frank and Robert Fenno, National Politics and Federal Aid to Education Syracuse, Syracuse University Press, 1962.

Munger, Frank J., "Opinion Elections, Parties and Policies : A Cross State Analysis", Paper presented at the Annual Meeting of the American Political Science Association held at New York on September 2–6 1969.

Murphy, Jerome T., State Education Agencies and Discretionary Funds, Lexington, D.C. Heath, 1971.

Murphy, Walter F., "Lower Court Checks on Supreme Court Power", American Political Science Review, 1959.

Myrdal, Gunnar, An American Dilemma, New York, Harper and Row, 1962.

Nachmias, David, Public Policy Evaluation, New York, St. Martin's Press, 1979.

Nadel, Mark V., The Politics of Consumer Protection, Indiana-Polis Bobbs Merrils, 1971.

Nadel, Mark V., "The Hidden Dimension of Public Policy : Private Governments and the Policy-Making Process, USA, Journal of Politics, February, 1975.

Nagel, Ernest, "The Enforcement of Morals" USA, The Humanities, No. 3, 1968.

Nagel, Thomas, "Equal Treatment and Compensatory Discrimination", USA, Philosophy and Public Affairs, 1973.

Narasimhan, V.K., Democracy and Mixed Economy, Bombay, Popular Prakashan, 1965.

Narasimhan, V.K. "The Concept of Margin in Politics", Smarajya 1965.

Nathan, Richard P., The Plot that Failed, New York, Wiley, 1975.

Nayar, P.B.K., Leadership, Bureaucracy and Planning in India, Delhi, Associated Publishing House, 1969.

Needler, Martin C., Political Systems of Latin America, Princeton, D. Von Nostranl, 1964.

Neibuhr, Reinhold, The Children of Light and the Children of Darnkess, New York, Charlis Scriber's Sons, 1945

Neustadt, Richard, Presidential Power, New York, Wiley, 1960.

Newbaner, Deane E., "Some Conditions of Democracy", American Political Science Review, 1967.

Newland, Cheater A., "Press Coverage of the United States Supreme Court," USA, Western Political Quarterly, March, 1964.

Newman, Peter, The Theory of Exchange, New Jersy, Prentice-Hall 1965.

Niederhoffer, Arthur, Behind the Shield, New York, Doubleday, 1967.

Nienaber, Jeanne and Aaron Wildavsky, The Budgeting and Evaluation of Federal Recreation Programmes : Or Money Doesn't Grow on Trees, New York, Basic Books, 1973.

Nisbet, Robert A., The Quest for Community, New York, Oxford University Press, 1953.

Noorani, A.G., "The Politics of Violence", Indian Express, November 30, 1966.

Nordlinger, Eric A., The Working Class Tories, Berkeley, University of California Press, 1967.

North, Douglas C., and Roger Leroig Miller, The Economics of Public Issues, New York, Harper and Row, 1971.

Oaks, Dallin, "Studying the Exclusionary Rule in Search and Seizure", University of Chicago, Law Review, 1970.

O'Brien, Lawrence, No Final Victories, New York, Ballentive, 1975.

Olson, Mancur, Jr., "Rapid Growth as a Destabilizing Force", USA, Journal of Economic History, December, 1963.

Olson, Mancur, The Logic of Collective Action, Cambridge, Harvard University Press, 1971.

O'Neil, Robert M., "Racial Preference and Higher Education : The Larger Context, USA, Virginia Law Review, 1970.

Oppenhiem, Felix, Dimensions of Freedom : An Analysis, New York, St. Martin's Press, 1961.

Oppenheim, Felix, Moral Principles in Political Philosophy, New York, Random House, 1968.

Optner, Standford L., Systems Analysis For Business and Industrial Problem Solving, New Jersy, Prentice Hall, 1965.

Orfield, Gray, Congressional Power : Congress and Social Change, New York, Harcourt Brace Jovanovich, 1975.

Orfield, Gray "Congress, the President and Anti-Busing Legislation, 1966-1974", USA, Journal of Law and Education, 1975.

Organski, A.K.A., The Stages of Political Development, New York, Algerd, A. Knopf., 1965.

Oxenfeldt, Algred, and Vsevolod Holubochy, Economic Systems in Action, New York, Holt Rinehart and Winston, 1965.

Page, Benjamin I., and Richard A. Broody, "Policy Voting and the Electoral Process, American Political Process, American Political Science Review, 1972.

Paranjape, H.K., "Political and Administrative Problem of Implementing the Indian Journal of Public Administration, October, 1963.

Parenti, Michael, Democracy for the Few, New York, St. Martin's Press, 1963.

Passell, Peter, "The Detereent Effect of the Death Penalty : A Statistical Test", USA, Stanford Law Reviews, November, 1975.

Paulson, Monard G., "DeFunis : The Road Not Taken", USA, Virginia Law Review, 1974.

Peabody, Robert L., and Nolson W., Plosby, New Perspectives on the House of Representations , Chicago, Rand McNally, 1969.

Peabody, Robert L. (*et al.*), To Enact A Law, New York, Praeger 1972.

Pearsons, Talcott, "The Political Aspect of Social Structure and Process" in Easton David (ed.), Varieties of Political Theory, New Jersy, Prentice Hall, 1966.

Pechman, Joseph A., and P. Michael Timpane (eds.), Work Incentives and Income Guarantees, Washington D.C., Brookings Institution, 1975.

Peltason, Jack W., Federal Course in the Political Process, New York, Random House, 1955.

Penniman, Clara, "The Politics of Taxation" in Jacob, Herbert, and K.N., Vines (eds.), Politics in American States, Boston, Little and Brown Company, 1976.

Pennock, Roland, "Democracy is not Paradoxical", USA, Political Theory, February, 1974.

Peterson, American Labour Unions, New York, Harper and Row, 1963.

Pettigrew, Thomas F. (*et al.*) "Busing : A Review of the Evidence", USA, The Public Interest, 1973.

Pffifner John M., and Frank P. Sherwood, Administrative Organizations, New Jersy, Prentice Hall, 1960.

Pierce, Lawrence, C., The Politics of Fiscal Policy Formation California, Good Year, 1971.

Pierce, Neil R., "State Local Report : Structural Reforms of Bureaucracy Grows Rapidly", USA, National Journal, 1975.

Piven, Frances Fox, and Richard A. Cloward, Regulating the Poor, New York, Pantheon, 1971.

Plott, Charles, "Axiomatic Social Change Theory : An Overview and Interpretation", USA, American Journal of Political Science, 1976.

Pomper, Gerald M., Elections in America : Control and Influence in Democratic Politics, New York, Dodd and Mead 1973.

Popper, Karl, The Logic of Scientific Democracy, New York, Harper and Row, 1959.

Pressman, Jeffrey L., and Aaron B. Wildavsky, Implementation Berkeley, University of California Press, 1973.

Prothro, J.W., and C.M., Grigg, "Fundamental Principles of Democracy : Bases of Agreement and Disagreement", in Cnudde, C.F., and D.E. Neubauer (eds.), Empirical Democratic Theory, Chicago, Markham, 1969.

Fryor, Fredrick, Public Expenditure in Capitals and Communist Countries Illinois, Irwin, 1968.

Pulsipher, Alan G., and James L. Weatherby, "Malapportionment, Party Competitions, and the Functional Distribution of Government Expenditure", American Political Science Review, 1968.

Pye, Lucian W., "Introduction : Political Culture and Political Development", in Pye and Verba (eds), Political Culture and Political Development, New Jersy, Princeton University Press, 1965.

Pye, Lucian W., Aspects of Political Development, Boston, Little and Brown Company, 1966.

Quade, E.S., Analysis for Public Decisions, New York, American Elsevier, 1975.

Radcliffe—Brown, A.R., Structure and Functions in Primitive Society, New York, Free Press, 1957.

Rae, Douglas, "Maximin Justice and an Alternative Principle, American Political Science Review, 1975.

Rahman, A., "New Tasks Need New Machinery", Citizen and Week—end Review, July, 1969.

Rahman, A., "Science Policy in India", Lokudyog, May, 1969.

Ranney, Austin (ed.), Political Science and Public Policy, Chicago, Markham, 1968.

Rapoport, Anatol, Fights, Games, and Debates, Ann Arbor Mihigan University of Michigan Press, 1960.

Rapoport, Anatol, and Albert Chammah Prisoner's Dilemma Ann Arbor Michigan, University of Michigan Press, 1965.

Rawls, John, The Theory of Justice Cambridge, Harvard University Press, 1971.

Rawal, John, The Justification of Civil Disobedience" in Beauchamp, Tom (ed.), Ethics and Public Policy, New Jersy, Prentice–Hall, 1975.

Reagen, Micheal D., (ed.), The Administration of Public Policy, Illinois, Foresman and Company, 1969.

Redford Emmette S., Ideal and Practice in Public Administration Tuscalossà, University of Albama Press, 1958.

Redford, Emmette S., Democracy in Administrative State, New York, Oxford University Press, 1969.

Redford, Emmette S., The Regulatory Process, Austin, University to Texas Press, 1969.

Reedy, George E., The Twilight of the Presidency, New York, New American Library, 1970.

Rein Martin, Social Science and Public Policy, Pennsylvania Offset Paperback Mfrs., 1976.

Rejai, M. (ed.), The Contemporary Theories of Democracy, New York, Atherton Press, 1967.

Rapass, David E., "Comment : Political Methodologies in Disarray", American Political Science Review, 1976.

"Report of the President's Committee on Administrative Management", USA, 1937.

Report of the Committee on the Training of Civil Servants", London, H.M.S.O., 1944.

Riggs, F.W., the Ecology of Public Administration New Delhi, Indian Institute of Public Administration, 1961.

Riker, William, The Theory of Political Coalitions, New Haven, Yale University Press, 1963.

Riker William and Peter Ordershook, An Introduction to Positive Political Theory, New Jersy, Prentice Hall, 1973.

Riker, William and Steve Brams, "The Paradox of Vote Trading', American Political Science Review, 1973.

Ripley Randell B., and Grace A. Franklin, Congress, The Bureaucracy and Public Policy, Illinois, Dorsey, Dressy, 1976.

Rischer, Nicholas, Distributive Justice, Indianapolis, Bobbs—Merrill 1966.

Rischer, Nicholas, Introduction to Value Theory, New Jersy, Prentice Hall, 1969.

Rischer, Nicholas, Welfare : The Social Issue in Philosophical Perspective, Pittsburgh, University of Pittsburgh Press, 1972.

Rivlin, Alice M., Systematic Thinking for Social Action, Washington D.C., Brookings Institution, 1971.

Robinson, Michael J., "Public Affairs, Television and the Growth of Political Malaise", American Political Science Review, 1976.

Robinson, Michael, "Television and American Politics", U.S.A., The Public Interest, 1977.

Rogers, Harrell R. Jr., and Charles S., Bullock, Law and Social Change, New York, McGraw–Hill, 1972.

Rose, Richard, Policy Making in Great Britain London, MacMillan, 1969.

Rosen, Paul the Supreme Court and Social Science, Chicago, Universityof Illinois Press, 1972.

Rosenan, James R. (ed), Domestic Sources in Foreign Policy, New York, Free Press, 1967.

Rosenbaum, Walter A., The Politics of Environmental Concern, New York, Praeger, 1973.

Rosenberg, M.J. (*et al.*), Attitude Organization and Change, New Haven, Yale University Press, 1960.

Ross, Arthur, M., "The Data Game" in Peters, Charles and John Rothchild (eds.), Inside the System, New York, Praeger, 1973.

Rothenberg, Jerome, The Measurement of Social Welfare, New Jersy, Prentice Hall, 1961.

Rostow, W.W., The Process of Economic Growth, New York, Norton 1962.

Rourker, Frencis E. (ed.), Bureaucratic Power in National Politics, Boston, Little and Brown Company, 1965.

Rourke, Francis E., Bureaucracy, Politics and Public Policy, Boston, Little and Brown Company, 1969.

Royoko, Mike, "Few Seem to Care If Teacher Cheat", USA, New Orleans Time—Picayunl, January, 1977.

Russett, Bruce M., "Inequality and Instability," USA, World Politics, April, 1964.

Russett, Bruce M. (*et al.*), World Handbook of Political and Social Indicators, New Haven, Yale University Press, 1964.

Sabine, G.H., and T.L. Thorson, A History of Political Thought, Tokyo, Halt Saunders, 1963.

Saha, Meghand Rethinking Our Future, Calcutta, Indian Science News Association, 1954.

Salisbury, Robert, "The Analysis of Public Policy", A Search for Theories and Roles" in Ranney, Austin (ed.), Political Science and Public Policy Chicago, Markham, 1968.

Samuelson, Paul, "The Pure Theory of Public Expenditure", USA, Review of Economics and Statistics, 1954-55.

Samuelson, Paul, "A Diagrammatic Exposition of a Theory of Public Expenditure", USA, Review of Economics and Statistics, 1954–55.

Samuelson, Paul, "Aspects of Public Expenditure Theories", USA, Review of Economics and Statistics, 1958.

Schaaffer, G.F., and Stuart Rakoff, "Politics, Policy and Political Science", USA., Politics and Society, 1970.

Schattschneider, E., The Semi–Soverlign People, New, York Holt, Rinehart and Winston, 1960.

Schelling, Thomas, The Strategy of Conflict, New York, Oxford University Press, 1963.

Schllesingér, Arthur M., A Thpusand Days, Boston, Houghton Mifflin,1965.

Schiller, Marvin, "On the Logic of Being a Democrat" USA., Philosophy, 1969.

Shculman, Paul R., "Nonincremental Policy Making : Notes Toward and Alternative Paradigin", American Political Science Review, 1975.

Schultz, Charles, The Politics and Economic of Public Spending, Washington D.C., Brookings Institution, 1968.

Seidman, Harold, Politics, Position, and Power, New York, Oxford University Press, 1975.

Seifer, Ncy, Nobody Speaks for Me, New York, Simon and Schuster, 1976.

Selznick, Philip, "Institutional Vulnerability in Mass Society", American Journal of Sociology, 1951.

Sen, Amartya, Collective Choice and Social Welfare, San Francisco, Holden-Day, 1970.

Sessums, T. Terrell, "Legislating a Growth Policy", USA, State Government : Journal of State Affairs, 1974.

Shah, A.B. (ed.), The Great Debate, Bombay, Lalvani Publishing House, 1968.

Shah, A.B., Planning for Democracy and Other Essays, Bombay P.C. Manaktala & Sons, 1967.

Shapiro, Martin (ed.), The Supreme Court and Public Policy, Illinois, Scott, Foresman and Company, 1969.

Sharkansky, Ira, Policy Analysis in Political Science, Chicago, Markham, 1970.

Shaw, D.C., and M.E., McCombs (eds.), The Emergence of American Political Issue, New York, West, 1977.

Shills, Seaward, A., "The Torment of Secrecy, Illinois, Free Press, 1955.

Sigal, Leon V., "Official Secrecy and Informal Communication in Congressional—Bureaucratic Relations", U.S.A., Political Science Quarterly, 1975.

Sills, David L., International Encyclopedia of Social Sciences, New York, Free Press, 1968.

Simon, Herbert, Administrative Behaviour, New York, MacMillan, 1947.

Simon, Herbert, "Notes on the Observation and Measurement of Political Power", USA, Journal of Politics, 1953.

Simon, Herbert, "A Behavioural Model of Rational Choice", USA, Quarterly Journal of Economics, 1955.

Simon, Herbert, "Theories of Bonded Rationality", in McGuire, C.B., and R. Rander (eds.), Decisions and Organizations, Amsterdam, North-Holland, 1972.

Singh, V.B., Essays in Indian Political Economy, Bombay, People's Publishing House, 1967.

Skinner, Quantum, "The Empirical Theorists of Democracy and their Cutics", U.S.A., Political Theory, 1973.

Smith, James Ward, Theme for Reason, New Jersy, Princeton University Press, 1957.

Smith, M.B. (*et al.*), Opinions and Personality, New York, John Wiley and Sons, 1964.

Smith, T. Alexander, The Comparative Policy Process, California, Clio Books, 1975.

Somit, Albert, and Joseph Tanenhaus, The Development of American Political Science : From Burges to Behaviouralism, Boston, Little and Brown Company, 1967.

Sorensen, Theodore C., Decision Making in the White House, New York, Columbia University Press, 1963.

Sorenson, Theodore C., Watchmen in the Night, Massachusetts, MIT Press, 1975.

Sorzano, J.S., "David Easton and the Invisible Hand", American Political Science Review, 1975.

Sorzano, J.S., "Values in Political Science : The Concept of Allocation", USA, Journal of Politics, 1977.

Sowell, Thomas, "Affirmative Action Reconsidered", USA, The Public Interest, 1976.

Spanier, John and Eric M. Uslaner, How American Foreign Policy is made, New York, Holt, Rinehart and Winston, 1979.

Srinivasan, N., Democratic Government in India, Calcutta, World Press, 1954.

Steinbrunner, John D., The Cybernetic Theory of Decision, New Jersy, Princeton University Press, 1974.

Steiner, Gilbert Y., Social Insecurity : The Politics of Welfare, Washington, Bookings Institution, 1966.

Steiner, Gilbert Y., The State of Welfare, Washington D.C., Brookings Institution, 1971.

Stokes, Donald E., and Warren E. Miller, "Party Government and the Saliency of Congress", USA, Public Opinion Quarterly, 1962.

Stokey, Edith, and Richard Zeckhauser, A Primer for Policy Analysis, New York, Norton, 1978.

Stone, Alan, Economic Regulation and the Public Interest, Ithaca, Cornell University Press, 1972.

Stone, Clarence N. (*et al.*), Urban Policy and Politics—In a Bureaucratic Age, New Jersy, Prentice Hall, 1979.

Straayer, John A., and Robert D. Wrinkle, American Government Policy, and Non-Decision, Ohio, Merrill, 1972.

Strauss, Leo, What is Political Philosophy? Illinois, Free Press, 1959.

Strom, Gerald, "On the Apparent Paradox of Participation : A New Proposal", American Political Science Review, 1975.

Sullivan, John L., and Robert E. O'Connor, "Electoral Choice and Popular Control of Public Policy", American Political Science Review, 1972.

Sundquists, James L. Politics and Policy, Washington D.C., Brookings Institution, 1968.

Sundquists, James L., On fighting Poverty, New York, Basic Books, 1969.

Synder, R.C., and James A. Robinson, National and International Decision-Making, New York, Institute for International Order (Undated).

Tacheron, Donald D., and Morris K. Udall, the Job of Congressmen, New York, Bobbs—Merrill, 1966.

Tanehaus, Joseph (*et. al.*), "The Supreme Court's Certiorari Jurisdiction : The Theory", in Schubert, Glendon (ed.), Judicial Decision-Making, New York, Free Press, 1963.

Tao, L.S., "The Need for a Morally Based Decision on Capital Punishment", USA, Notre Dame Lawyer, April, 1976.

Tawney, R.H., Equality, New York, Allen and Unwin, 1952.

Taylor, Charles, "Neutrality in Political Science", in Laslett, P., and W.G. Runciman (eds.), Philosophy, Politics, and Society, New York, Barnes and Noble, 1967.

Taylor, Michael, Anarchy and Cooperation, New York, John Wiley and Sons, 1976.

Teller, Edward, Hans Mark, and John S. Foster, Power and Security, Lexington, D.C. Health, 1976.

Thomas, Norman C., Education in National Politics, New York, McKay, 1975.

Thompson, Victor, Bureaucracy and Innovation, Tuscaloosa, University of Albama Press, 1969.

Thorson, Thomas, The Logic of Democracy, New York, Holt, Rinehart and Winston, 1962.

Tisdel, Clem, "Concepts of Rationality in Economics, USA, Philosophy and Social Science, 1975.

Titmus, Richard M., Income Distribution and Social Change, Toronto, University of Toronto Press, 1962.

Toulmin, Stephen, Reason in Ethics, Cambridge, Cambridge University Press, 1960.

Tufte, Edward R., Political Control of the Economy, New Jersy, Princeton University Press, 1978.

Tufte, Edward R., "The Relationship between Seats and Votes in Two-Party Systems", American Political Science Review, 1973.

Tullock, Godon, Toward a Mathematics of Politics, Ann Arbor, Michigan, University of Michigan Press, 1967.

Tumin, Melvin M., Desegregation : Resistance and Readiness, Princeton, Princeton University Press, 1958.

Turner, Henry, "How Pressure Groups Operate", Annals of the American Academy of Political Science and Social Science, Philadelphia, USA., 1968.

Ulmer, Sidney S., "Earl Warren and The Brown Discipline", USA, Journal of Politics, 1971.

Uslaner, Eric, and J. Ronnie Davis, "The Paradox of Vote-Trading Effects of Decision Rules and Voting Strategies on Externalities", American Political Science Review, 1975.

Vakil, C.N., "The Human Factor in Economic Development", Commerce, September 1961.

Van Horn, Carl E., "Implementing CETA : The Federal Role", Paper Presented at the Annual Meeting of the Midwest Political Science Association held at Chicago on April 29—May 1, 1976.

Verba, Sidney, and Norman Nie, Participation in America, New York, Harper and Row, 1972.

Verney, Doughlas V., An Analysis of Political Systems, London, Routledge and Kegan Paul, 1959.

Vladeck, Bruce C., "Why Non-Profits Go Broke", USA, The Public Interest, 1976.

Wade, L.L., and R.L. Curry Jr., A Logic of Public Policy, California, Wadsworth, 1970.

Wade, Larry L., The Elements of Public Policy, Ohio, Merrill, 1972.

Wahlke, Heinz Elau, W. Buchanan, and L.C. Ferguson, The Legislative System, New York, John Wiley and Sons, 1962.

Walker, Jack, "A Reply to "Further Reflections on the Elitist Theory of Democracy", American Political Science Review, 1968.

Walker, Jack, "The Diffusion of Innovation Among the American States", American Political Science Review, 1969.

Walton, Richard E., and Robert B. McKersie, A Behavioural Theory of Labor Negotiations, New York, McGraw-Hill, 1965.

Wasby, Stephan L., Political Science, Calcutta, Scientific Book Agency, 1972.

Watts, Harold M., "Graduated Work Incentives", American Economic Review, 1969.

Webber, Melvin M., "The BART Experience—What Have We Learned"? USA, The Public Interest 1971.

Weber, Max, The Methodology of Social Sciences, Illinois, Free Press, 1949.

Weber, Max, Economy and Society, New York, Bedminister Press, 1968.

Weber, Ronald E., Public Policy Preference in the States, Indiana, Institute of Public Administration, Indiana University, 1971.

Wechsler, Herbert, "Toward Neutral Principles of Constitutional Law", USA, Harvard Law Review, 1959.

Weiss, Carol, Evaluating Action Programmes, Boston, Allyn and Bacon, 1972.

Weiss, Donald, "Rejoineder", USA, Political Theory, 1973.

Wholey, Joseph S., Federal Evaluation Policy, Washington D.C., Urban Institute, 1970.

Wicksteed, Philip H., The Common Sense of Political Economy, London, MacMillan, 1950.

Wildavsky, Aaron, The Politics of Budgetary Process, Boston, Little and Brown Company, 1964.

Wildavsky, Aaron, "Rescuing Policy Analysis from PPBS", USA., Public Administration Review, 1969.

Wildavsky, Aaron, Speaking Truth to Power, New York, Wiley 1979.

Wilensky, Herold, and Charles Lebeaux, Industrial Society and Social Welfare, New York, Free Press, 1965.

Wilensky, Herold, Organizational Intelligence, New York, Basic Books, 1967.

Wiliam, Walter L., Social Policy Analysis and Research, New York, American Elesevier, 1971.

Wilson, Bryan (ed.), Rationality, New York, Harper and Row, 1970.

Wilson, James Q., and Edward C., Banfield, "Public Regardiness as a value Premise in Voting Behaviour, American Political Science Review, 1964.

Wilson, James Q., Thinking about Crime, New York, Basic Books, 1975.

Wise, David, The Politics of Lying, New York, Vintage, 1973.

Wolman, Harold, Politics of Federal Housing, New York, Dodd and Mead, 1971.

Wood, Robert, "When Government Works", USA, The Public Interest, 1970.

Woodward, Bob, and Carl Bernstein, All the Presidents Men, New York, Simon and Schuster, 1974.

Woodward, Bob, and Carl Bernstein, The Final Days, New York, Avon Books, 1977.

Young, Roland (ed.), Approached to the Study of Politics, Evanston, Northwestern University Press, 1958.

York, Herbet F., Race to Oblivion, New York, Simon and Schuster, 1970.

Ziegler, Harmon, Interest Groups in American Society, New Jersy, Prentice-Hall, 1964.

Zimring, Franklin E., "Firearms and Federal Law", USA, Journal of Legal Studies, 1975.

INDEX

A

Almond, 20
Almond, G.A., 19, 20, 110
Aristocracy, 3-5
Aristocratic families, 22
Aristotle (father of Political Science), 2
Articulation of interest, 23
Austin, 4
Authoritative allocation of values, 17, 18

B

Black-box of Easton, 110
Britain, 85, 86, 88
British Institute of Public Administration (BIPA), 31
Bureaucracy, 126

C

Central administration, 5
Central pay commission, 30
Chandigarh's transfer to Punjab, 123
China, 83
Chinese communist party, 83
Church, 47
Classification of government, 3
Cobb, 118, 119
Components of the policies, 48
Concept of political system, 66
Congress in U.S.A., 83
Congress Party, 7, 88
Congress-I government, 120
Constitution of India, 88

D

Democracy, 3-5, 89, 91
District state, 5
Dye, Thomas R., 8, 120, 178

E

Easton, David, 16, 17, 66, 68
Elder, 118, 119
Elite theory, 58
Elites, 92
England, 83
Environment, 75, 109
Executive policy prevails, 85

F

Family, 47
Founder of communism, 2
France, 85

G

Gandhi, Indira, 7, 119, 120
Green, T.H., 4
Groups of people, 79

H

Hereditary criteria, 22

Hobbes, 3
Hoover Commission, 30

I

Identification of the problems, 117-118
Incremental model, 54
India, 83, 85
Indian Institute of Public Administration (IIPA), 31
Input-output model, 20
Iriedrich, Carl J., 8

J

Janata government, 7
Japanese Cabinet, 85
Jones, Charles O., 34

L

Labour union, 47
Local finance enquiry commission, 30
Lok Sabha, 84

M

Marx, Karl, 1, 4, 93
Mass media, 24, 169
Mobocracy, 5
Models of public policy, 47-71
approaches of public policy, 51-52
benefits and losses, 49
boundaries of the political systems, 67
boundary, 66
choices are made and why, 49
components, 48
defence, 50
descriptive model, 55-56
deterministic model, 56
difference does moneymake, 50
education, 50
elite model, 57-58
functional model, 61
group model, 62
impact of public policy, 50
implications, 59-61
application, 61
appraisal, 61
intelligence, 61
invocation, 61
prescription, 61
recommendation, 61
termination, 61-62
input, conversion, output, 67
institutional model, 56
issued in policy analysis, 49
policy analysis is evaluation, 51
normative model, 56
political system, 66
probabilistic model, 56
rational model, 53-54
social welfare, 50
sub-system, 66
system bodel, 64-65
utility of model, 70-71
verbal model, 56
Monarchies, 3-5
Montesquieu, 4

N

National Security Act (1933), 87
Natural Gas Commission, 31
Notions of political equality, 92

O

Oligarchy, 3, 5

P

Para-military, 36
Parliament in Britain and India, 83
Parliamentary form of political systems, 82, 84
People's republic of China, 85
Police, 1, 36
Policies of law and commerce, 39
Policy evaluation, 160-180
  direct costs terms of resources devoted to the programme, 167
  impact of public policy, 164-165
  impact on future as well as immediate conditions, 166-167
  impact on situations or groups, 166
  impact on the target situation or group, 165-166
  indirect costs, including loss of opportunities, 167
  limitations, 178
  policy evaluation four concepts, 171-173
    efficiency, 172-173
    equity, 171-172
    pareto optimality, 173
    public interest, 174-175
  policy evaluation problems, 175-177
  policy impact, 168-169
  problems, 176
  public policy limitations, 178-179
Policy formulation, 109-135
  executive and bureaucracy, 127-128
  identifying policy agenda, 117-119
  identifying policy problems, 110-113
  legislature-bureaucracy interaction, 126-127
  legislature-executive interaction, 124-125
  policy decisions, 128-129
  policy problems and elites, 115-116
  policy proposals, 121-123
  styles of decision-making, 130-131
    bargaining, 130-131
    command, 131-132
    competition, 131
    conflict, 132
    co-operation, 132-135
Policy implementation, 137-158
  authority, 146-147
  courts, 141
  implementors inclination, 147
  information, 145-146
  interest groups, 141
  legislature, 140-141
  problems of implementors, 141-143
    communication, 141-142
    resources, 144
  public-negative approach, 153-158
  public-positive approach, 148-149
  staff, 144-145
Policy of education, 37
Political equality, 92
Political recruitment, 22
Political socialisation, 21, 22

Polybins, 3
Position of legislatures, 83
Principle of popular sovereignty, 91
Problems, 112
Public opinion, 24, 112
Public policy and environment, 74-105
  administrative agencies, 85-86
  citizen, 104-105
  courts, 87-88
  democratic political system expresses, 95
  governmental policy-making agencies, 81-83
    legislatures, 82
    executive, 83-84
  information, 95
  interest group techniques, 101
  lobbying, 101-102
  non-governmental policy making agencies, 95-97
    political party, 96-97
    interest groups, 97-98
  political culture, 75-76
    parochial political culture, 76-77
    participant political culture, 77-78
    subjects political culture, 77
  political equality and political freedoms, 92-93
  popular sovereignty, 91-92
  propositions, 80-81
  public policy and democracy, 88-89
  set of a interactions, 78
  social and economic factors, 78-79
  strike, 103-104
  system capacity, 93-94
Public policy, 1-41
  assumptions public policy, 34
  basic concept of state, 2
  basis of policy formulation, 29-31
    external sources, 30
    internal sources, 29-30
    research and survey, 30
    special investigations, 30
  definitions, 7-9
  dilemmas of policy-making process in India, 31-33
    absence of systematic study and research, 32
    departmentalism, 33
    evils of bureaucracy, 31-32
    poor implementation, 31
    tenure system under stress, 32
  discipline, 2
  elections, 6
  feed back model, 28-29
  input functions, 20-21
    political socialisation and recruitment, 20-21
    role of education, 21
    – – elders, 21
    – – environment, 21
    – – equals, 21
    – – friends, 21-22
    – – married life, 22
  input-output structures, 19-20
  interdisciplinary field of inquiry, 1
  interest aggregation, 24

interest articulation, 23
nature, 9-10
objectives, 12
output functions, 25-27
policy analysis, 33
political communication, 24-25
politics and policy, 14-15
politics and policy: politics as an activity, 15
problems and demands, 35
regulatory, 37
rule-enforcing, 26
rule-interpreting, 27
rule-making, 26
stages, 10-11
policy control, 12
– education, 11
– formulation, 11
– implementation, 11-12
– interpretation, 11
types of objectives, 12-14
long term, 13
political, 14
professional, 14
scientific, 13
short term, 13
types of public policy, 36-38
– – appeal, 40
– – capitalization, 38-39
– – development policies, 40
– – distributive, 38
– – ethical, 39
– – externally imposed policies, 41
– – ideological, 39-40
– – implied, 41
– – macro economic, 40
– – original, 40
– – redistributive, 38
– – sectoral, 40
– – substantive, 36
Public utility services, 37

R

Rational policy-making, 54
Rose, Richard, 8
Rule enforcing, 27
Rule interpreting, 27

S

Secret police, 27
Social governance, 5
Societal groups, 47
Spencer, Herbert, 4
Stone, Robert Eye, 7
Supreme Soviet, 83

T

Totalitarian political system, 100
Tyranny, 5

U

U.S.A., 83, 86, 87, 102, 115, 122
Constitution, 93
U.S.S.R., 83, 85
University grants commission, 30

V

Value allocations, 18

Z

Zoological Surveys of India, 31